ALSO BY JAMES BISHOP

Bruce Lee: Dynamic Becoming

~

Who Wrote the Tao? The Literary Sourcebook for the Tao of Jeet Kune Do

REMEMBERING BRUCE LEE

His Enduring Legacy and Inspiration

25th Anniversary Edition

James Bishop, Ph.D.

PROMETHEAN PRESS™
Dallas   Vancouver

Published by Promethean Press™
A division of Promethean Multimedia, LLC
Dallas, TX
www.promethean-press.com

Copyright © 2024 by James Bishop

All rights reserved, including the right of reproduction
in whole or in part in any form.

Originally published in 1999 under the title *Remembering Bruce:
The Enduring Legacy of the Martial Arts Superstar*

Images in the chapter "What if Bruce Lee Had Lived?" unless
otherwise indicated, were partially produced using Midjourney AI.

Manufactured in the United States of America

Hardcover Edition: ISBN 978-1-77331-008-4
Paperback Edition: 978-1-965522-00-4
E-Book Edition: 978-1-965522-01-1

For Bella and Connor

Acknowledgments

The author would like to thank and acknowledge the following people: *James and Martha Bishop, Vanessa Izaguirre, Cynthia Izaguirre, Jose Fraguas and Mark Kimora of CFW Enterprises, John Little, Melanie Shapiro at Cyclone Books, Larry Hartsell, Debra Hartsell, Lamar M. Davis II, Burton Richardson, Steve Golden, Patrick Strong, Jon Benn, Grace Lui and the South China Morning Post, Judith Singer and Warner Brothers, Victor Maldonado at Globe Photos, Linda Lee Cadwell, Taky Kimura, Martin O'Neill, Alex Shunnarah, Joe Hyams, Bob Bremer, Leo Fong, Richard Torres, Mark Cole, Daniel Lee, Robert Blakeman, Jeff Chinn, Ray Van Pelt, Boyd Thomas, Anand Upadhyaya, Dr. George James, Michael Shahim, Dith Hat, David DiPietro, and Gerald Markee.*

Table of Contents

Preface to the 2024 Edition
1

Introduction
5

Bruce Lee: A Brief History
11

Bruce Lee: Martial Artist
15

Bruce Lee: Philosopher
33

Bruce Lee: Movie Star
43

Bruce Lee: Family Man
61

Bruce Lee: Human Being
67

Bruce Lee: Legend
77

The Legacy of Bruce Lee
83

What If Bruce Lee Had Lived?
173

Out of the Darkness of Our Ignorance
181

Appendix

Recommended Resources
190

Bibliography
195

Index
198

PREFACE

It's hard to believe that it has been a quarter of a century since *Remembering Bruce: The Enduring Legacy of the Martial Arts Superstar* was first published.

In February 1999, I was approached to write a book on Bruce Lee. At the time, I was developing a reputation as a writer for *Black Belt* and *Inside Kung Fu* magazines. My article "Bruce Lee and the Taoist Connection", the first article I wrote that specifically focused on Bruce Lee, was featured in the current issue of *Inside Kung Fu* magazine. I also hosted *Everything About Bruce Lee* – at the time the most popular Internet forum on the subject of Lee.

Melany Shapiro of the California-based publisher Cyclone Books was seeking to add a book on Bruce Lee to her publishing catalogue and, being aware of my scholarship on the subject due to the *Inside Kung Fu* article currently on the newsstands, reached out to me to gauge my interest in being the author. Of course, I was interested, and on February 28th I submitted my proposal to Cyclone Books. They loved it.

"Your proposal looks terrific," wrote back Melany Shapiro on March 3rd. "I can send you a contract right way." However, the deal came with a catch: while I had the freedom to make the book I wanted to make, the book had to be completed and in the editor's hands by the end of March. That was an incredibly tight deadline to write an entire book.

Also complicating the situation was that I needed to conduct interviews with people who knew Bruce Lee to compile the information for the book. Making those contacts, arranging interviews, and writing the entire book in a month's time would be impossible. The Jun Fan Jeet Kune Do Nucleus annual meeting, a public conference featuring a number of original students, family, and friends of Bruce Lee, was in late April and offered the best opportunity to gather information from a number of sources in one weekend. After explaining to Shapiro the challenges of the timeline, she agreed to extend the deadline to the first week of May, provided I had the first three chapters of the book completed and submitted by the end of March.

Throughout the month of March, I spent my time productively writing the preliminary chapters and completing as much of the later chapters as I could accomplish with my previously-conducted research. I interviewed several key individuals over the phone, including Seattle-era student Patrick Strong, Los Angeles-era student Larry Hartsell, and John Little, the Bruce Lee estate's literary executor and the primary person driving the reconsideration of Bruce Lee as a philosopher. I also arranged licensing arrangements for the photographs that were used in the book.

In April, I flew out to Seattle to attend the Jun Fan Jeet Kune Do Nucleus conference (the organization would be rebranded as

The Third Annual Jun Fan Jeet Kune Do Conference provided a unique opportunity to meet Bruce Lee's family, friends, and students in one event. From left to right: Daniel Lee, Steve Golden, Shannon Lee, Taky Kimura, George Lee, and Linda Lee Cadwell. (Author's archives)

the "Bruce Lee Educational Foundation" after the event) and gathered the information I needed. Over a three-day period, I attended talks by a number of associates and family members of Bruce Lee, trained with some of his students, and snagged several critical interviews. During that weekend, I also met many Bruce Lee fans from all over the world, made many lasting friendships that endure to this day, and met the men who would become my formal Jeet Kune Do instructors when I returned to Dallas.

During a ceremony at the gravesite of Bruce and Brandon Lee, Linda Lee Cadwell, Bruce Lee's widow, approached me. She surprised me when she said, "You're James Bishop, aren't you?" Mrs. Cadwell knew of me because I was corresponding with the attorney for the Bruce Lee Estate, Adrian Marshall, and also because of a conversation she had with John Little, who, after our interview, discussed my project with her. She told me she would like to get together with me that weekend and talk. Later at the hotel, we sat down and discussed my plans for the book. After providing the details of the tone and direction of my book, Linda Lee Cadwell wished me well on my project and offered me access to the Lee family photograph library, should I need it. I thanked her for the offer, but I ultimately chose not to accept the access to Lee family photographs out of concern that it might come with strings attached.

Remembering Bruce was released in the Fall of 1999. In April the following year, I received an award for my essay "On Totality" at the Bruce Lee Educational Foundation's annual conference in Las Vegas. After receiving the award,

Meeting Linda Lee Cadwell at the gravesite of Bruce Lee on April 24, 1999. (Author's archives)

Posing for photos with Bruce Lee Educational Foundation director John Little, Shannon Lee, and Linda Lee Cadwell after receiving my writing award at the Bruce Lee Educational Foundation Annual Conference on April 29, 2000. (Author's archives)

Linda Lee Cadwell greeted me as I came down from the stage. She congratulated me on my award then took to the stage and addressed the audience. "I just wanted to mention that James Bishop has written a book called *Remembering Bruce* that I have read," she said, "and I think it is a very fine book, so congratulate him on that as well."

Remembering Bruce has long been out of print and over, the years, I fielded many questions about its availability, with most asking me if it would ever be reprinted. For a long time, I resisted the urge to republish *Remembering Bruce*, but I have finally consented to its republication with this revised 25th anniversary edition (retitled *Remembering Bruce Lee* to put a finer point on it). Everything has been reviewed and updated to reflect the most current knowledge on Bruce Lee. This book was a product of my youthful optimism, and I am happy to make the book available to a new generation of Bruce Lee fans.

James Bishop, Ph.D.

INTRODUCTION

What's the big deal about Bruce Lee? I can't begin to count the number of times I have been asked that question. Inevitably, as people get to know me, they come to find out that I have a particular interest in the subject of Bruce Lee. This revelation is usually followed by pseudo-Bruce Lee *wataahh!* impressions and mock martial arts fighting stances. I have learned to accept this with good humor, but answering their question is not so simple. To most people, Bruce Lee was a kung fu movie star, a short sidenote in entertainment history, and someone who lived and died before their memories began. Little thought is given to the historical significance of the man himself.

Bruce Lee was much more than just a simple movie star. Lee was an excellent example of a 20th century renaissance man. He was an author, scholar, teacher, philosopher, and groundbreaking martial artist whose creative energy and desire to grow brought him the admiration of hundreds of thousands of people. Bruce Lee's impact on the world was just beginning when his life abruptly ended on July 20, 1973.

It's impossible for me to explain the importance of Bruce Lee without going into a little detail about my own life, of which I'll be brief.

I was one of those people who, for the first 22 years of my life, thought that Bruce Lee was just some kung fu actor. I never sat through a Bruce Lee movie, and the brief glimpses I had of him on television hadn't impressed me, since I had little interest in the martial arts. As a child, my father enrolled me in karate classes, but I quit after receiving my first belt because I simply wasn't interested. After high school, I spent the next few years trying to figure out what to do with my life. An artist and a writer, I yearned to make a living as one or both, yet I was paralyzed by my own fear of failure and the idea that such endeavors were impractical, a viewpoint reinforced by society. I could not reconcile my own creative impulses with the need to build a practical future for myself. I was torn, and I was getting nowhere in life.

In 1993, I had finally decided to choose a path. I enrolled at the Art Institute of Dallas. Very soon, I realized I had made a big mistake. The monotonous, joyless "art" I was being trained to produce (for what would be the rest of my life) was sucking the pleasure of the craft right out of me. I realized I was facing a future career that I would grow to hate. I found myself right back where I was. It was, at this point, that my life completely changed.

Intrigued by a movie trailer for *Dragon: The Bruce Lee Story*, I went to see it the first night it was released. Sitting in the darkened theater with my date, I became mesmerized by the life story of Bruce Lee. This man was everything I admire in humanity: a thinker, philosopher, lover, warrior, and friend. He was a seeker of the truth,

While not exactly historically accurate, the movie Dragon; The Bruce Lee Story *portrayed a version of Bruce Lee that left an impression on the author.* (© 1992 Universal Pictures)

Dragon: The Bruce Lee Story accurately captured Bruce Lee's probing intelligence, sense of optimism, and openness to experience. (© 1992 Universal Pictures)

fought against racism and, most importantly, made the conscious decision not to be bound by the limits society and tradition placed upon him. Never had I experienced a persona so dynamic, so full of life. *This man lived!* I mean, he didn't just live, he *lived*.

As my date and I left the theater, I was charged with an excited energy I never felt before. I told her that I was going to take up the martial arts. She laughed and said I wasn't the first guy she had seen come out of an action movie temporarily pumped up, that it was just the testosterone talking. She underestimated the effect the movie had on me. To this day, I still have the movie ticket stub, as a reminder of the day my life changed.

The next day at the Art Institute, I was talking to my classmates about my experience and my desire to study the martial arts. The thirty-something classmate sitting across the table from me mentioned that he was a black belt in Taekwondo and Shotokan and would be interested in putting together a small class at his home, if I was interested. I was, but I explained to him that I didn't have much money. He responded by saying that he wouldn't be doing it for the money and that, as long as I came and put in the effort, he wouldn't charge me. When six others expressed interest in his class, he invited them as well. In retrospect, fate seemed to be playing a hand in my life.

He trained us earnestly. Our backyard meetings were conducted rain or shine. Being from the "old school," his lessons were a matter of physical hardship and practicality. Sparring was an integral part of our program, even as beginners, and he was primarily concerned with the real-world applications of the techniques. He was also quick to give sage advice on life in general: how to be a man, a husband, a father; how to treat others, and how to demand respect for yourself.

Over time, the other students dropped out of the class, but I continued to study under the same instructor, and he became one of my very best friends. I am sure that my experience echoes the experience of many of Bruce Lee's original students, most of whom have shared similar experiences with Bruce Lee.

I left the Art Institute of Dallas in the Fall. I realized that the trade school was not compatible with my goals and needs; that, much like a single martial art style, it was too restrictive and did not allow me the opportunity to grow in other areas that I wished to explore: writing, philosophy, and history. I enrolled in a university to get a more comprehensive education.

After seeing the movie *Dragon: The Bruce Lee Story*, I became extremely well informed on the subject of Bruce Lee. I watched, read, and analyzed every bit of information available on Lee. I found his theories of Jeet Kune Do not only applicable to martial arts, but to life as well. I discovered Taoism, which brought me further spiritu-

The author's training with Sensei Boyd Thomas was physically challenging and focused heavy on sparring and practical combat applications. (Author's archives)

Inspired by Bruce Lee's philosophical journey, the author left art school to study writing and philosophy at a university. (Author's archives)

al and mental enrichment. And I discovered that the real Bruce Lee is even more fascinating than the one in the movie.

Using Lee as an example, I persevered in my dream of becoming a writer. My first professional sale was in the September 1997 issue of *Black Belt Magazine*, a magazine for which Bruce Lee himself once wrote. It was an article on role models in the martial arts. Though I chose to focus on currently living martial artists, including Bruce Lee's student Dan Inosanto, my biggest role model was Bruce Lee, for it was the light of his life that illuminated mine.

Said Bruce Lee historian John Little, the author of *The Warrior Within* and the editor of *The Bruce Lee Library Series*, "Bruce is a role model. Particularly for young males, speaking from my own experience. But I also think that Bruce's ability as a role model cuts across genders, just as it cuts across nationalities, ethnic groups, and social classes. He has proven himself (for over five decades) to be a person who motivates individuals to achieve greater things; things that even they themselves initially may not have thought they had within them. But he awakens that, awakens the dragon within or the warrior within, if you will. He represents, to me (and I think to many people), the paragon of human achievement in mind, body, and spirit."

Editor-in-Chief David Granger wrote in the November 1998 issue of *Esquire*, "People want to believe in heroes but are having a harder time finding them." As a society, we look for examples of humanity that comprise the best aspects of the human ideal. I came to discover, quite by accident, that Bruce Lee was one such person.

Burton Richardson, a Jeet Kune Do instructor and writer, is amazed by the effect Bruce Lee still has on people. "I am surprised at how vast is Bruce Lee's fame. I was in a Zulu village in a remote part of South Africa to learn about their culture and to train in the Zulu stick fighting methods. After a few days, the translator showed the young men I was training with a magazine, which had one of my articles in it. He was explaining what I did in the Zulu language. I couldn't understand what he was saying, but when he said 'Bruce Lee' the warriors all said *'ahh'* with tremendous respect. Bruce Lee had passed away before these men were born, yet out in that village in the middle of the Zulu nation, Bruce Lee was a hero."

This isn't simply another biography on Bruce Lee. This is more of a meditation on Lee, part biography and part exploration of the many ways that he inspired people throughout the world. In the pages that follow, you will learn many things about the Little Dragon, but you will also read the stories of people, like me, who were changed by Bruce Lee, whether directly (as in the case of his family, friends, and students) or indirectly (as in the case of his fans).

My personal experience is similar to that of many Bruce Lee fans around the world. There is something about his charisma, drive, and imagination that touches something in everyone. You can worship a Tom Brady, a Robert Downey, Jr., or a Beyonce, but will such celebrities ever affect the way you look at the world or how you see yourself? Whereas stars such as these are more concerned with getting a bigger swimming pool, Lee was concerned with getting the bigger picture. He was intent on doing more than become a successful movie star. Bruce Lee wanted to change the world.

BRUCE LEE: A BRIEF HISTORY

My majoring in philosophy was closely related to the pugnacity of my childhood. I often asked myself these questions: What comes after victory? Why do people value victory so much? What is "glory"? What kind of "victory" is "glorious"?

Bruce Lee

Bruce Lee's story began on November 27, 1940, at the Jackson Street Hospital in the Chinatown district of San Francisco, in the Chinese year of the dragon, hence his life-long association with dragon mythology. Lee's father, Lee Hoi Chuen, accompanied by his wife, Grace, was an actor touring in America with the Cantonese Opera Company. Bruce Lee's Chinese name, *Jun Fan*, which means "return again", was given to him by his mother, a prophetic act considering her child would one day return to the land of his birth to pursue his destiny. It was a nurse in the hospital who chose the name "Bruce" for Lee, putting it on his birth certificate.

A few months after his birth, Bruce Lee's parents returned to their home in Hong Kong with the new addition to the family. The infant appeared in his first film, *The Golden Gate Girl*, before he and his family even left San Francisco.

At the age of six, Bruce Lee began appearing in a series of movies, beginning with *The Birth of Mankind*. He was billed as *Lee Siu Lung* (Lee Little Dragon). Lee usually played orphans and juvenile delinquents in his childhood movies. He appeared in at least 20

In re:

LEE JUN FON, alias BRUCE LEE, native born citizen of the United States, for citizen's Return Certificate, Form 430. (Male)

••••••••••••••••••••••••••••

State of California)
City and County of) ss
San Francisco)

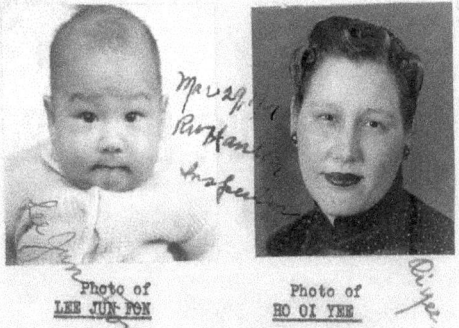

Photo of
LEE JUN FON

Photo of
HO OI YEE

HO OI YEE, being first duly sworn, deposes and states as follows:

That she is a temporary resident of the United States; that she was duly admitted to the United States by the United States Immigration Authorities at the Port of San Francisco, California, incident to her arrival from China, ex SS "President Coolidge", on the 8th day of December, 1939, No. 39707/8-25;

That she is the mother of LEE JUN FON, alias BRUCE LEE, who is applying for a citizen's Return Certificate, Form 430, at the Port of San Francisco, California; that the said LEE JUN FON, alias BRUCE LEE, was born in the United States;

That affiant has attached her photograph and that of her said son, LEE JUN FON, alias BRUCE LEE, hereto for the purpose of identification;

That your affiant makes this affidavit for the purpose of aiding her said son, LEE JUN FON, alias BRUCE LEE, in obtaining a citizen's Return Certificate, Form 430.

Ho Oi Yee

Subscribed and sworn to before me
this 5th day of March, 1941.

Notary Public in and for the
City and County of San Francisco,
State of California.

National Archives at San Francisco
Case File 12017/53752, RG 85

Even though Bruce Lee's parents were only temporarily in the United States for work purposes, Lee's birth in San Francisco in 1941 guaranteed his right to United States citizenship.

such movies during his childhood, including *Kid Cheung* and *The Orphan*.

Bruce Lee attended LaSalle College (a sort of preparatory school) starting at the age of 12. He was a rambunctious and energetic child who was often disruptive in class. Outside of school, Lee often got into fights with boys from various gangs and cliques around Hong Kong. Because of these conflicts, he convinced his mother to let him take martial arts classes (without his father's immediate knowledge or approval), and, at the age of 13, Bruce Lee enrolled in the kwoon (martial arts school) of Professor Yip Man, head of the Wing Chun style of gung fu (*gung fu* is the Cantonese spelling which Lee preferred over the Mandarin *kung fu*).

Bruce Lee had a taste for fighting, which the study of gung fu failed to alleviate. He'd keep a steel chain hidden around his waist, anticipating trouble. Lee continued to get into fights, most importantly to test the skills he had learned from his gung fu studies. Like most Chinese in Hong Kong, Bruce Lee and his friends deeply resented the British colonial rule, and they often picked fights with the bigger British boys from neighboring King George V school. As a result, he became well known to the police of Hong Kong.

Bruce Lee was a very popular child among his peers, especially with the young girls. A great dancer, Lee was crowned the Hong Kong Cha Cha champion in 1958. He was not, however, a very good student. Lee saw no real value in formalized education and focused his attention on his study of Wing Chun, leaving little energy for his academics. Furthermore, he was openly defiant against the teachers and administrators of LaSalle College. Eventually, he was expelled from LaSalle.

Bruce Lee enrolled at St. Francis Xavier High School. His family hoped a change of venue would improve his behavior, but it did little to improve things. Lee was still combative in his attitude toward others. Though he dreamed of becoming a doctor, his continued poor performance in school was making that an impossibility. One of his teachers, Brother Edward, recognized Bruce Lee's gift for fighting and encouraged him to enter the 1958 Interschool Boxing Championships. The boxing championship was held under European Queensberry rules. Lee progressed into the finals where it came down to him against, Gary Elms, a British boy from King George V High School. Elms was a three-time champion defending his title for a record fourth year.

Bruce Lee made it to the finals with relative ease, but Gary Elms gave him trouble. Lee fought in a typical Western fashion of boxing, and he finally encountered a boxer who was better at it than him. Feeling that he was losing the fight, Lee switched to his Wing Chun techniques and gained the upper hand, winning the bout by knockout in the third round.

A group altercation between his fellow Wing Chun students and the students of a Choy Li Fut gung fu school was the boiling point in Bruce Lee's teenage troubles. The fight was prearranged and took place on an apartment building rooftop in Kowloon Tong, a Hong Kong suburb. As Lee was taking off his jacket, his opponent sucker-punched him in the eye. The infuriated Lee exploded, beating the boy with a series of straight punches before kicking him in the eye and mouth, knocking him out. The boy suffered a broken arm and a missing tooth.

The boy's parents filed a grievance with the police and Bruce Lee's mother was forced to go to the police station and sign a paper guaranteeing her son's good conduct. The police began to suspect that Lee and his friends were gang members.

Since Bruce Lee was born on American soil, it was decided, for his sake, that he should go to America and claim his citizenship. Lee's mother, Grace, believed that going to America would not only give him the opportunity to finish his education, but also, at the rate things were going, likely keep him alive.

After going through some difficulties with the immigration service because of his suspected gang activities, Bruce Lee was cleared to leave. He left Hong Kong in April 1959, boarding a steam ship to America with little more than a few personal items and a hundred dollars. Before embarking on his voyage, Bruce Lee's father did something that he would normally never do – *he gave his son a hug*. When Lee left, his father told his mother, "All he's got is US $100 in his pocket. I hope he makes it."

BRUCE LEE: MARTIAL ARTIST

To me, ultimately, martial arts mean honestly expressing yourself. To express oneself honestly, not lying to oneself -- that, my friend, is very hard to do.

Bruce Lee

Though he studied for five years under Sifu Yip Man, Bruce Lee's evolution as a martial artist did not begin until he was in America. It was in the great melting pot of the USA that Lee would be exposed to new ideas, new martial arts, and new challenges.

Bruce Lee stayed for a short time in San Francisco, the city of his birth, upon arriving in the United States. He eventually settled in Seattle, Washington, taking a job at family friend Ruby Chow's Chinese restaurant. He enrolled at Edison Technical High School, where he earned his high school diploma. While there, Bruce Lee gave a gung fu demonstration as part of an Asian celebration. A gang of neighborhood toughs, the Capitol Hill Gang, were in the audience. Their leader, a big, muscular man named James DeMile, age 20, was unimpressed by the slight Chinese man's fancy movements and animal forms. DeMile was a heavyweight boxing champion in the Air Force and was familiar with fighting. As he was thinking to himself, Bruce Lee turned to the audience and, as if reading his thoughts, said, "You look like you can fight. How about coming up here for a minute?"

DeMile, who had never been defeated in boxing or in streetfights, was undaunted by Bruce Lee's challenge. He stepped up and stood toe-to-toe with Lee.

The challenge was simple. DeMile simply had to connect with a punch in whatever manner he chose to throw it. DeMile shot out a right that Bruce Lee blocked easily. Lee immediately followed up with a left that stopped just short of DeMile's nose. What followed was more of the same. When DeMile tried to connect, Lee evaded or parried the blow and then followed up with his own, just stopping short of his target but making it obvious that he could have done some damage. To add insult to injury, Lee ended the demonstration by rapping DeMile on the head and asking if anyone was in there.

"He embarrassed me," remembered DeMile. "He didn't even give me the courtesy of working up a sweat."

After the demonstration, DeMile approached Bruce Lee and convinced him to give DeMile and his friends fighting lessons. Lee began regularly instructing them in gung fu in the alley behind Ruby Chow's restaurant.

Shortly thereafter, a local grocer named Taky Kimura was introduced to Bruce Lee. "Ed Hart was shopping in my store," remembered Kimura. "He said, 'Look! You've got to meet this guy! He's 18 years old!'"

Kimura decided to accept Ed Hart's invitation, and one Sunday he went to where they were training. "It was always their practice that, if they brought somebody in, they would put you up against Bruce and say, *'Do something!'*" Kimura threw a punch at him. "He had me tied up and I could feel the punches stop short of hitting me right against my face. I could feel that wind, just hitting me in my face. *It scared the Hell out of me!* I thought, *'Geez, I've got to learn this!'*" Kimura joined the class. He would later become Lee's senior student in Seattle.

Bruce Lee was very opinionated about the essence of martial arts and was not afraid to voice those opinions. He sought the company of other martial artists but often angered them with his "presumptuous" views. "There are those that have said that Bruce was very cocky and abrasive, but so many times I was with Bruce, and someone would come up to him and say, *'What is your style?'*" said Kimura. "They'd talk a little bit, and Bruce would say, *'Well, I'd do this...'* and the guy would say, *'Oh yes, we have that, too, you know!'* Bruce would realize that any further confrontation would end up in a fight, so he'd say, *'Oh God, you must have a great system!'*

Staff members at the First Hill Food Center, 908 8th Avenue in Seattle, celebrating the store's grand opening with a group portrait in the produce section. The store was owned by brothers Taky and Eiji Kimura. Taky Kimura (last on the right) was Bruce's Lee's friend and senior student during the martial artist's Seattle years, and for decades gave free weekly classes on Jun Fan Gung Fu in the Food Center basement. Photo by Albert J. Smith, Sr. (MOHAI, Al Smith Collection)

and turn and walk away."

At one demonstration in Seattle, a second-degree black belt from Japan named Uechi took exception to some of Bruce Lee's comments and challenged him. Lee assured him that his comments were not meant to be taken personally, but the man refused to back down. Uechi was present at some of Bruce Lee's previous public appearances and taunted him. Lee reluctantly accepted his challenge, and the entire group moved to a nearby handball court.

The karate practitioner opened with a kick that Bruce Lee easily blocked. Lee then followed up with a series of straight punches in rapid succession, forcing the karate stylist back the entire length of the handball court and finished him off with a kick to the head. The fight was over in 11 seconds. The karate man wasn't even given an opportunity to defend himself. When he asked, in a semi-conscious stupor, how long he had lasted against Bruce Lee, DeMile lied and told him, "Twenty-two seconds," doubling the actual figure.

"Ah," said the karate man, seemingly pleased with his performance. He then passed out.

In an effort to explain his bruised and battered face, Uechi later told his friends that he was involved in a car accident. Bruce Lee never made it a point to correct him. He never held a grudge. In fact, Lee allowed the karate stylist to join his class, though Uechi only lasted a short time.

Bruce Lee told Taky Kimura, "Look, we're not going to teach this guy too much because he's a smart ass."

At the first class he attended, the karate stylist pointed to the older Kimura and asked Bruce Lee, "You think I can beat Kimura?"

"Bruce said, *'Hell no, he'd kick your butt,'*" said Kimura, "which I couldn't have done. That's the kind of guy Bruce was way back then. He was very tolerant."

Bruce Lee's classes could be a very grueling experience. "A couple of guys fainted, a few threw up," recalled Patrick Strong. "They were hard, hard workouts."

Bruce Lee never asked of his students anything that he didn't expect of himself. Lee's personal practice was equally intense. He spent a great deal of his training time practicing on the *mook jong* (wooden dummy) used by Wing Chun practitioners to develop their hand skills. "When he worked that wooden dummy, it was just frightening," recalls Kimura. "You could hear it blocks away. It was like it was a big earthquake or something."

Bruce Lee developed his now famous "One-Inch Punch" by 1963. The punch was a demonstration of his ability to generate maximum power in a minimum of movement. At a demonstration of gung fu at Garfield High School in Seattle, Lee invited the biggest kid in attendance to participate in his demonstration. Bruce Lee explained that he was going to put his fist on the towering young man's chest and, just by twitching his body, send the boy flying backwards. Lee placed a chair several feet behind the boy to catch him when he flew back. The teens in the audience smirked incredulously.

Bruce Lee placed himself in front of the youth and extended his arm until it was a mere one inch from the boy's solar plexus. Lee told the young man to brace himself, which the boy did, despite being sure that the slight Chinese man could not move him. Bruce Lee twitched his body, slightly jerking the shoulder of his extended arm toward the boy, who went flying back more than five feet, landing in the chair Lee left for him. The gathered students let out a collective gasp.

"I began learning Gung Fu at 13, because I wanted to learn how to fight," Bruce Lee told the students. "Now it has changed my whole life, and I have a completely different way of thinking. I

Bruce Lee and Sheldon Wong giving a martial arts demonstration on an outdoor stage in Seattle's Chinatown (now the International District) after the Chinese Community Night parade on August 3, 1961. Photo by Yuki. (MOHAI, Seattle Post-Intelligencer Photograph Collection)

want to establish gung fu institutes throughout the United States and write books about it."

Bruce Lee's gung fu technique was already evolving, whether he realized it or not. "It started as just a natural progression of logical moves that eliminated a wasted motion here and a wasted motion there, introduced a move that worked a little better here and there," said the late Ed Hart, one of Bruce Lee's first students. "I don't know at what point he realized he wasn't even doing Wing Chun anymore."

Bruce Lee finally opened an official gung fu school in the fall of 1963. It was located a short distance from the University of Washington, where he was a drama major. The gung fu school enabled him to leave the Chinese restaurant and became his home as well as his source of income. He called his martial art *Jun Fan Gung Fu*, after his childhood name. The school did reasonably well and by June of 1964, Bruce Lee made plans to open a second school with friend and fellow gung fu stylist James Lee in Oakland, California. He left his school in the hands of Taky Kimura and moved south.

Bruce Lee was invited to give a demonstration at the August 1964 International Karate Tournament in Long Beach, California. The tournament was the creation of Ed Parker, himself a Kenpo karate stylist and one of the most influential martial artists of his time. At the tournament, Bruce Lee made his entrance dressed in a black gung fu uniform and spoke a few moments about his martial arts. He then demonstrated his gung fu forms and *chi sao* (sticking hands) exercises, which he performed blindfolded with a partner. The highlight of his performance was again his "One-Inch Punch" which he performed in front of hundreds of seasoned martial artists. After Lee finished, there was momentary silence and then the crowd showered him with enthusiastic applause. Interestingly, Bruce Lee would get a similar audience reaction when he attended the premiere of his first martial arts movie, *The Big Boss*.

Bruce Lee's appearance at Kenpo master Ed Parker's (pictured) 1964 Long Beach tournament would prove to be life-changing for Lee.

One of the martial artists in attendance was Dan Inosanto. Inosanto, a student of Ed Parker, was very impressed by Bruce Lee's display. Lee was equally impressed with Inosanto. When Inosanto was point sparring, a referee failed to see a strike he landed against his opponent, one which should have earned him a point. Bruce Lee came up to Inosanto after the match and told him that he had seen Inosanto strike his opponent, but that he had moved too fast for the referee's eyes. That night, Inosanto met with Lee and a friendship was forged. Because of his talent and background in the martial arts (he had trained in Kenpo, Kali, and Escrima), Inosanto became Bruce Lee's principal student in Los Angeles and served as his sparring partner at tournament demonstrations.

During this time, Bruce Lee married his girlfriend from Seattle, Linda Emery, and the couple moved in with his business partner and friend, James Lee.

Bruce Lee was making a name for himself in the Oakland area, and that was both bad and good. Although he was attracting students in the community with his martial arts demonstrations, he was also attracting unwanted attention. Lee's boasting and cocky criticisms of the way the martial arts were currently being practiced and taught in the community offended many teachers – most of whom were traditionalists. Instructor T. Y. Wong, for example, who went through an acrimonious professional split from James Lee at the same time that James Lee jumped ship to become Bruce Lee's student, referred to Bruce Lee as a "dissident with bad manners." To make matters worse, Bruce Lee all but challenged anyone in the local martial arts community to find him at his school if they wanted to test his Wing Chun. The elders were very upset, and something had to be done about it.

Sometime between late December 1964 and early January 1965, a letter was hand-delivered by the local Chinese martial arts community to Bruce Lee at his Jun Fan Gung Fu Institute. Inside the school, the messenger found Lee, his wife Linda, and James Lee. The letter requested a challenge fight between Bruce Lee and Shaolin stylist Wong Jack Man, who just immigrated from China. Bruce Lee agreed to the fight and, after some back and forth over the course of days, a date for the fight was set for November.

On the date scheduled, Wong Jack Man arrived with a handful of witnesses. According to Linda Lee, Bruce Lee turned to Wong Jack Man and calmly asked him if this was what he wanted. Wong Jack Man said no, but that he was obligated to follow the wishes of the community. Lee nodded in agreement.

Perhaps surprised that Bruce Lee fully intended to go through with the fight, the delegation from the Chinese community whispered among themselves for a few moments. They then tried to back off of their original challenge, suggesting a "friendly" sparring match instead. Bruce Lee would have none of it and exploded with anger.

"No! You challenged me, so let's fight!"

"Alright," said one of the delegates. "But no kicking in the groin.

Wong Jack Man at the premiere of the 2016 flim Birth of the Dragon, *which told Wong's version of the fight with Bruce Lee.* (Getty)

No hitting in the face."

"I'm not standing for any of that!" replied Bruce Lee. "You came here with a challenge, hoping to scare me off. You've made the challenge – so I'm making the rules. As far as I'm concerned, it's no-holds-barred. It's all out!"

This left Wong Jack Man with no choice but to fight or lose face. The combatants prepared to fight and bowed formally to each other.

What followed has been disputed by both camps. According to Wong Jack Man, Bruce Lee offered a friendly hand and when Wong attempted to accept it, Lee tried to gouge Wong Jack Man's eyes. Wong managed to avoid the eye jab. Bruce Lee began fighting in typical Wing Chun fashion and the challenger responded in his Northern Shaolin style. At first their different styles had the effect of canceling each other out, creating a stalemate that lasted a couple of minutes. Wong Jack Man was spinning and moving, making him very hard to hit. Lee tried to land a barrage of chain punches that were consuming a lot of his energy. Wong Jack Man claimed that Lee made continuous, serious attempts to gouge Wong's eyes and puncture his throat.

"He really wanted to kill me," recalled Wong.

In Linda Lee's version of events, by the third minute, Bruce Lee began to get the upper hand. Wong Jack Man's entourage tried to step in, but James Lee held them back. The fight took a comical turn, with Wong Jack Man running around the room trying to escape Bruce Lee, who continued to punish him with a steady stream of blows to the back of his head and back. Finally, Lee was able to get his arm around Wong Jack Man's neck and took him to the ground, where Lee pummeled him until Wong Jack Man gave up. Bruce Lee threw the whole group out of his school, and they left in silence.

Wong Jack Man disputed that version of events. Wong claimed

that the fight lasted at least 20 minutes, and Wong managed to get Bruce Lee in a headlock three times. He claims he did not submit to Lee, and the fight ended in a stalemate.

"I had dinner with Bruce shortly after his fight with Wong Jack Man," said Bruce Lee student Patrick Strong. "He told me how he went after Man with chain punches but had a hard time landing because Wong Jack Man kept running and spinning. Bruce's punches just weren't landing the way he wanted them to. Finally, he threw him down and kept punching. At the time Bruce told me the story, he sounded very pleased with himself."

Regardless of who emerged as the victor of the fight (or if there was even a victor at all), Bruce Lee was, in reality, extremely disappointed in his performance. A fight that should have taken a few seconds (like his previous altercations) had taken three minutes. Lee found that not only had his Wing Chun been unsatisfactory, he barely had enough physical endurance to earn the victory. Bruce Lee was exhausted and short of breath.

This was a turning point for the martial art of Bruce Lee. He came to realize that his style of gung fu was too restrictive. Wing Chun was primarily composed of close infighting punches with little in the way of kicks or distance strikes, which was hardly of any use against Wong Jack Man's long-form gung fu. Wing Chun was not the complete answer, and there was no "effective segment of totality". Stylistically, Wing Chun restricted him. Bruce Lee would need to go beyond Wing Chun if he wanted to succeed in the future. In addition, he would have to condition his body to be prepared for another such encounter. Never again would Bruce Lee be caught at less than peak performance. It was on this day that the roots of Bruce Lee's Jeet Kune Do, of "having no way as way", were born.

With the help of James Lee, who was a weightlifter and physical fitness enthusiast, Bruce Lee began a regimen of intense physical conditioning. For his endurance, he would run three miles a day then ride an exercise bike to the point of exhaustion. For his strength training, Bruce Lee developed a program of weightlifting and resistance training that was specifically geared to gain him "real world power", namely, strength that would augment his fighting skills and not necessarily for aesthetic beauty. Bruce Lee placed special importance on strengthening the abdomen, "the real source of power" (as Lee described it) and the place that needed to withstand punishing body strikes. He also emphasized strengthening the forearms, which gave him additional power in his punches. Bruce Lee developed forearms that were unbelievably big and were larger than his biceps (which he felt would restrict his punching power if he built up too much). He began to record and monitor his progress in notebooks.

With his martial art, Bruce Lee began to take a scientific approach to training. Realizing that all knowledge had intrinsic value, Lee began to read and study about other martial arts. He would scour the local used bookstores, buying books on every combative principle he could find, from styles such as western boxing or French Savate to books on European fencing and Greco-Roman wrestling. Lee did not limit his studies to just combat principles. He bought books on psychology and motivation, medicine and kinesiology, philosophy, and religion. His personal library exceeded 2,500 books. Anything that could possibly help him in a fight or enrich his evolution, not just as a martial artist, but as a human being, was of value.

Bruce Lee would also study the work of famous boxers, such as Jack Dempsey and Joe Louis, watching old movie reels and analyzing their movements and executions. Lee especially liked Muhammad Ali's unconventional style of boxing, particularly the footwork, which Lee absorbed into his own personal expression of fighting. "He really liked Muhammad Ali because of the lightness of the footwork," said Dan Inosanto. "He had a huge boxing film collection. I remember it used to drive me blind. It's not like video." Inosanto said Bruce Lee would often get excited reviewing the fight footage. "*'Oh, look at this! Come here, Dan, look at this! Isn't that fantastic?'* Sometimes I'd fall asleep!"

Bruce Lee placed an increased emphasis on physically sparring with other martial artists, because he felt that it was the single most important of aspect of training. Lee likened the concept of *kata*, pre-arranged forms that most karate practitioners practice alone, as not unlike "trying to learn to swim on dry land." Bruce Lee believed only against a real opponent could the martial artist prepare himself for the realities of combat. He would exchange ideas and information with his peers in the martial arts community, asking them to "show me what you know", mastering it himself after a few attempts, and then improving on it, much to the consternation of his fellow martial artists.

Said Joe Lewis, the "Muhammad Ali" of karate tournament fighters and a student of Bruce Lee's: "If you throw a punch or throw a kick, in my personal opinion, the purpose of that technique is to do damage. Well, Bruce Lee had the same philosophy, so we hooked up like that *[crosses fingers]*."

Some of the most important departures Bruce Lee made from conventional combat involved the lead punch and the stop-hit. Conventional thought is that the lead or forward hand is used to set up the punches of the back hand, which has further to travel and, as the wisdom goes, can generate more power in that time. Bruce Lee proved with his One-Inch Punch that a lead hand strike could produce the required power in a minimum of distance. "Bruce felt that the front hand, being closest to the target, was going to be doing 80% of the hitting," said Lee's student Jerry Poteet, "so it had to be developed to perfection. Instead of adding techniques or movements, he wanted us to refine the ones that were efficient."

The *stop-hit* was an important change Bruce Lee made in his martial art. The stop-hit (a concept from fencing) is a hit timed to intercept the opponent's strike before it reaches its target. It requires quick reflexes and the ability to intuit the opponent's movements. Lee's use of the stop-hit is evident in his movies. In his fight with Chuck Norris in *Way of the Dragon,* Lee used the stop-hit to jam Norris' leg before he could connect with a kick. The stop hit is the "intercepting fist" in Jeet Kune Do.

One important aspect of Wing Chun that Bruce Lee retained was the *simultaneous attack and defense*. In most martial arts, it is common to divide the fighting action into two parts: blocking and striking. You are taught to block your opponent's blow with one action and strike him with another. With simultaneous attack/defense, one makes the block and response one movement. The attack could occur just before, right as, or just after the parry. Bruce Lee taught his students to block and strike in one motion, making the action much faster and more efficient.

Another aspect of Bruce Lee's art borrowed from fencing is the concept of *broken rhythm*. In broken rhythm, one is able to determine the opponent's rhythm of movement. By following the opponent's rhythm, he will unconsciously begin to fight in tandem with you and you can then alter your own rhythm, disrupting the opponent and his ability to successful engage you.

Bruce Lee began to reject the idea of "styles" of fighting completely. "I personally do not believe in the word 'style'," said Lee at the time. "Unless there are human beings with three arms and four legs, there can be no different style of fighting. Why is that? Because we have two hands and two legs. The important thing is: how can we use them to maximum effect?"

The effect of all the revised training methods and experimentation was to increase Bruce Lee's already considerable speed and fighting skills to almost preternatural levels. Lee soon began to have trouble finding decent partners with whom he could spar. His own students could no longer give him a challenge – *or even a workout,* for that matter.

Bob Wall, a karate tournament fighter, was asked by Bruce Lee to make a "man's bag" on which Lee could practice his kicks and punches. "Bob Wall told me that he thought Bruce was kind of a brash guy and he was going to try and put him in his place," said Taky Kimura. Wall made the most ridiculously big bag he could devise. At about four feet in diameter and weighing 300 pounds, Wall was sure the slight Bruce Lee would not be able to budge it.

"Then Bruce kicked that thing, and it flew up to the ceiling, and I think that made a believer out of Bob," said Kimura.

"That's not happenstance," Bruce Lee historian John Little points out. "That's someone who has a scientific mind and knows all about force production."

It was about this time that Bruce Lee secured the role of Kato on the television show *The Green Hornet*, produced by the same team that brought the campy *Batman* series to television. Though the series lasted only one season, it brought Bruce Lee professional exposure to the Hollywood. After it was canceled, Lee began to teach celebrity students his martial art of Jeet Kune Do, or the "Way of the Intercepting Fist", as he was now calling it. Some of his better-known students were Steve McQueen, James Coburn, Blake Edwards, Roman Polanski, Lee Marvin, James Garner, and Kareem Abdul-Jabbar.

Through his celebrity contacts, Bruce Lee managed to keep working in the entertainment industry. Stirling Siliphant, the Oscar-winning writer of the movie In the *Heat of the Night,* was another of Lee's Hollywood students. Siliphant hired Bruce Lee as the fight coordinator for *A Walk in a Spring Rain,* a movie he was producing. Lee flew to Tennessee for the filming. Two large stuntmen on the picture had a hard time accepting "the little Chinese guy" as their boss, dictating how they should fight. Siliphant arranged a demonstration to clarify the situation.

Bruce Lee took a foam kicking shield and had the biggest stuntman follow him out to the set's swimming pool, where he gave him the shield and had him stand three feet from the pool. Said Lee: "I'm

The Green Hornet *television series, starring Van Williams as the titular Green Hornet and Bruce Lee as Kato, his partner in crimefighting, premiered on the ABC network in 1966 and lasted one season.* (20th Century Fox)

going to stand in front of you and, with no warning, I'm just going to kick. I'm going to lift the airbag you're holding, and you can get into any position you want. I'll lift you from there out in the air and into the swimming pool." The stuntman bent down, braced himself, and both he and his buddy laughed. They were still laughing when Bruce Lee suddenly *exploded* – kicking the shield and sending the stuntman to the other end of the pool, almost passing it. Though they were no longer laughing, the second stuntman remained unconvinced, and so Bruce Lee gave him a similar lesson. Lee proved himself to the stuntmen and, from that point on, they did whatever he asked of them.

Bruce Lee became even more controversial in the martial arts community. Thanks to the *Green Hornet,* Lee was getting much more attention from the public about his martial art, and he was sharing his views. Bruce Lee became bolder in his opinion of the martial arts, stating that "90% of Oriental self-defense is baloney" and that the only thing a karate belt was good for was "to hold your pants up, and that's about it."

As a result, Bruce Lee became a source of great antagonism in the martial arts community. Ed Parker remarked: "When Bruce ridiculed people, he wasn't very tactful. He didn't pull his punches at all. You don't make friends by telling people their way of doing things is full of shit."

Taekwondo master Jhoon Rhee agrees. "There were a number of people who didn't like Bruce, but when you are as frank as he was, you cannot avoid offending people."

Bruce Lee's training had reached the point where some of his mechanically-inclined students began devising new devices with which he could train. His Wing Chun dummy, a wooden post with strategically placed appendages to simulate a human opponent, became the only thing he could put all his effort against. It had to be modified to suit his special needs.

Herb Jackson, one of Bruce Lee's students, recalled constructing many devices to Lee's specifications. "Bruce was so advanced in his defense that there wasn't anybody he could really train with. His skills were so refined that he could literally destroy people. He needed training equipment that could take him full force and not fall apart."

When asked if he was really as good as his reputation, Bruce Lee would say, borrowing a quote from boxer Floyd Patterson, "Well, if I tell you I'm good, you will say that I'm boasting. But if I tell you I'm not good, you'll *know* I'm lying."

Blake Edwards, a film producer and former Bruce Lee student, said: "Bruce was a braggart, in a way, but he never bragged about anything he wasn't capable of."

At the same time, the martial arts community was criticizing Bruce Lee for not competing in tournament fighting. Many martial artists thought it odd that he had such revolutionary views but never got into the ring to prove them. Lee, for his part, believed that his art of Jeet Kune Do was focused on streetfighting and the restrictions of sport would not allow its full expression – just as the restriction of style would not allow a fighter to be complete. So long as he was restricted from using biting, eye-gouges, and other dirty tactics, Bruce Lee was unwilling to step in the ring. In fact, to "prove" the validity of Jeet Kune Do would mean seriously maiming or killing his opponent, something that simply was not feasible to him.

Bruce Lee student Larry Hartsell recalled the difficulties of proving Jeet Kune Do's efficacy in the ring. "I fought in a San Francisco arena contest in 1969. It was a toughman contest, three-rounder, heavyweight, *Ultimate Challenge* and all that. The purse paid us a thousand dollars. Back in the sixties, that was a lot of money. Still is, as a matter of fact. I beat this guy, knocked him out of the ring. But I caught him one time, knocked him down, and while he was down, I kicked him twice. They disqualified me for one round. So, I lost by decision but actually won. The guy (the opponent) even came over to me and told me I won. *[Hartsell laughed]*'

Larry Hartsell understood the difficulties in applying Jeet Kune Do in regulated competitions. (Photo courtesy of Larry Hartsell)

Bruce Lee was furious that his fighter was disqualified. In response, *Black Belt Magazine* published a strongly worded letter from Bruce Lee in which Bruce voiced his and Hartsell's complaints about the outcome of the fight. Jeet Kune Do was simply meant to be an all-out, anything goes approach to fighting where kicking an opponent on the ground is not only permissible but recommended if it means that the opponent won't be able to get up and continue his assault.

"Bruce's favorite technique was the Biu Gee, or 'eye strike'," points out Patrick Strong.

"The whole idea of tournaments, Bruce called them 'contests of ego' because that's what it's about," said John Little. "'I'm better than you' and the only way to prove who is best is by dominating an opponent, rather than dominating yourself, which was what Bruce was trying to get across to them. The fact that people still get hung up on the idea that it is solely about dominating an opponent shows how little they grasp the true spirit of the martial arts. That's the most primary dimension of it."

According to what Patrick Strong was told by Bruce Lee, Lee's biggest problem with tournaments was what he perceived as an inability to flow from technique to technique. "He described sparring and tournaments as two chickens fighting. They would go out there and face each other and then one would go *Peck! Peck!* And the other would then go *Peck! Peck!* You know, taking little pecks at each other. That's how he described it."

Therefore, for these reasons, Bruce Lee was unfazed by the remarks of the tournament martial artists. Lee was confident in his abilities. "I have no fear of the opponent in front of me. I'm very self-sufficient, and they do not bother me. And should I fight – should I do anything – I have made up my mind that, baby, you had better kill me before I get to you."

Bruce Lee felt that the killer attitude was the key to success in combat. "The worst opponent you can come across is one whose aim has become an obsession. For instance: if a man has decided that he is going to bite off your nose no matter what happens to him in the process, the chances are he will succeed in doing it. He may be severely beaten up too, but that will not stop him from carrying out his objective. That is the real fighter."

Though the martial arts community as a whole was skeptical of his claims, there were a few who secretly knew better. Chuck Norris, Mike Stone, and Joe Lewis (the father of kickboxing) were the top three martial arts tournament and full-contact fighters of the late sixties and early seventies, and all three came to Bruce Lee for private training. They would meet with Lee once or twice a week and practice with him. With Joe Lewis especially, Lee would teach the tournament fighter his techniques and then Lewis would go into the ring and prove them successful; in one example, Lewis used the Jeet Kune Do double hook to knock out Greg Baines in the first kickboxing title match. Though Chuck Norris and Mike Stone have been reluctant to give Bruce Lee any credit for their success, Joe Lewis publicly acknowledged his debt to his teacher for helping make him the best kickboxer of all time. In fact, Lewis credits Bruce Lee with being the true inspiration for kickboxing.

"That's to Joe Lewis' credit," said John Little. "As much as you align yourself with the truth, it reflects positively on you. Those that tend to conceal it... *[pauses]* Well, at some point, when the truth comes out, they're the ones that suffer for it. Remember, Bruce didn't go to their houses, they came to his house."

"I met Bruce in 1967," said Joe Lewis. "We started working out together later that year, '67, '68, and some in '69. When I started working with Bruce, I won eleven consecutive grand championship titles without losing. I became invincible all of a sudden."

Chuck Norris, for his part, is quick to praise Bruce Lee for his skills. "Bruce Lee was a paradox," he wrote in his book *The Secret Power Within,* "a small man who could easily defeat a giant with skill, speed, and extraordinary power."

Jon Benn, who played the evil mob boss in Bruce Lee's movie *Way of the Dragon,* which also starred Chuck Norris, said, "I once asked Chuck if they were in a real fight to the death, who would win? Chuck said, without hesitation, *'Bruce, of course.'*"

"Judo" Gene LeBell was one of the premiere American martial artists of the 20th century, whom Chuck Norris has referred to as "the killer of killers". LeBell, who worked with Bruce Lee as a stunt-

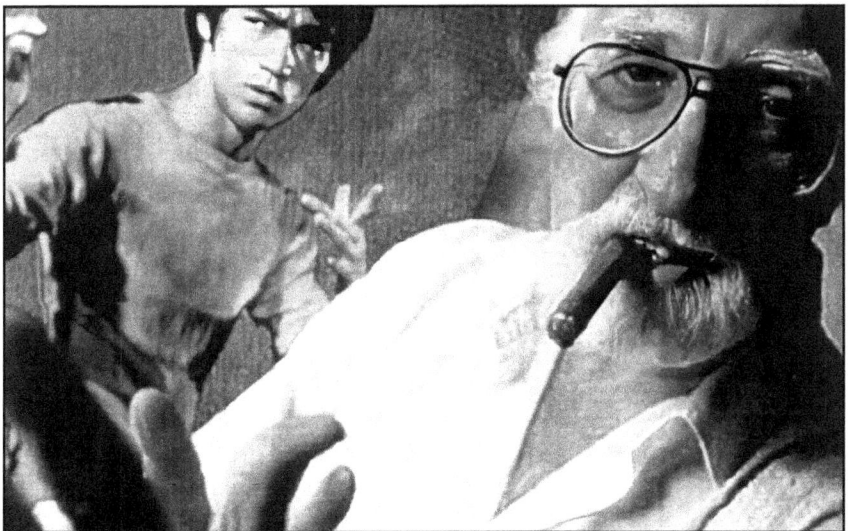

Jon Benn, Bruce Lee's co-star in the movie Way of the Dragon. (Photo courtesy of Jon Benn)

man on *The Green Hornet* series, said that Lee was the "best of his time."

One argument that Bruce Lee's detractors often make today is that Lee had poor grappling (ground fighting) skills and would have been in trouble against a wrestler or jujitsu artist. This false assumption was one that Bruce Lee himself appeared to encourage. "Bruce even had – what he kept very secret – plans to go from kicking range, boxing, trapping, all the way down to the ground and submission," said Larry Hartsell. "He had plans for that. He had them way back then when nobody even thought about it. He was prepared for that." The grappling that Bruce Lee displayed in his fight with Sammo Hung at the beginning of *Enter the Dragon* gives a hint to what Lee was capable of in terms of groundfighting.

Hartsell was not surprised at the people who have tried to downplay Bruce Lee's abilities since his death. Especially the statements of some of his contemporaries who were, interestingly, not so vocal when Lee was around to prove himself. "It could be anything," said Hartsell. "It could be their own ego. It could be their insecurities about themselves knowing what Bruce was. Anyone can talk about the dead, to build themselves up to be this and that."

Steve Golden, another of Bruce Lee's students, said, "I hear people now saying, 'Oh yeah, my instructor could do that' or 'I could beat Bruce'. They don't know. Everybody's talking. It's amazing that, after Bruce died, everybody got a lot better. It wasn't like that while he was alive. If you said you could beat him, he would be right in front of you."

For Jhoon Rhee, the truth was obvious. "I personally have never seen anybody, pound for pound, as strong as Bruce Lee. Now when he is no longer with us, it's pretty natural that there are some people who try to discredit Bruce. This does not change the actual facts. I know Bruce was a very good fighter."

BRUCE LEE: PHILOSOPHER

To me, all types of knowledge ultimately mean self-knowledge.

Bruce Lee

Bruce Lee's martial art could not have been as successful and complete without the deep philosophical base he gave it. Martial arts, by nature, are a reflective practice where the practitioner must not only examine the issues of life or death but also the nature of the self.

Bruce Lee's philosophical interests began when he was training in Wing Chun under Sifu (teacher) Yip Man. Yip Man put a great emphasis on the philosophical underpinnings of Wing Chun, and this had a great influence on Lee. Linda Lee Cadwell, Bruce Lee's widow, wrote in her book *The Bruce Lee Story:* "If there is anything that Yip Man gave to Bruce which may have crystallized Bruce's direction in life, it was to interest his student in the philosophical teachings of Buddha, Confucius, Lao Tzu, and other great thinkers and philosophers. As a result, Bruce's mind became the distillation of the wisdom of such teachers."

The single most important philosophical influence on Bruce Lee was his exposure to Taoist philosophy. Taoism is the development of the Chinese sage Lao Tzu, who, in the sixth century BC, wrote the definitive work on the subject, the *Tao Te Ching*. Taoism is identified by the Tai Chi, commonly referred to in the United States as the yin/yang symbol. At the heart of Taoist philosophy is man's relationship with nature. Lao Tzu believed that man is merely a part of a greater whole and, by accepting his relationship with the whole and following the course of nature with non-resistance, man can ultimately find success and serenity. Lao Tzu did not believe in a formalized system of education, nor did he believe in the Confucian doctrine of filial piety. Given Bruce Lee's troubles with schoolwork and teachers, it comes as no surprise that he felt a connection with Lao Tzu's message.

Taoism is often referred to as the *watercourse way*. A Taoist lives in harmony with nature and does not resist it. To that end, Taoists often cite water as an example of this concept. Water is infinitely flexible, goes around all obstacles, and can also be capable of tremendous power. To "be like water" is a critical philosophical lesson that Bruce Lee drew from his understanding of the Tao. It helped define his approach to combat and was a fundamental part of the ethos of Jeet Kune Do.

At the University of Washington in Seattle, Bruce Lee majored in drama but also took some philosophy classes. His grasp of Eastern concepts was impressive enough that he was sometimes asked to lecture on Eastern philosophy. In fact, it was during a lecture he gave at Garfield High School in Seattle that he met senior Linda Emery, who would one day become his wife.

"When he was in Seattle, Bruce used to quote Confucius and Lao Tzu and all those people like that, and he believed it," said Taky Kimura, Bruce Lee's senior student. "But pretty soon he made that transition himself and he *became the philosopher."*

In 1963, Bruce Lee self-published a book titled *Chinese Gung Fu: The Philosophical Art of Self-Defense*. The book expressed his views on gung fu as well as his deep interest in the philosophical aspects of martial arts training.

Bruce Lee was already beginning to feel discontent with "styles" of fighting. The idea did not follow the Taoist concepts of harmony and formlessness. On the separation between hard and soft styles of gung fu schools he said: "It's an illusion. You see, in reality, gentleness/firmness is one inseparable force of one unceasing interplay of movement. We hear a lot of teachers claiming their styles are either soft or hard; these people are clinging blindly to one partial view of the totality. I was once asked by a so-called 'kung fu master' – one of those that really looked the part with the beard and all – as to what I thought of Yin and Yang? I simply answered,

Bruce Lee was deeply influenced by the philosophy of Lao Tzu. (Photo courtesy of the South China Morning Post)

'Baloney!' Of course, he was quite shocked at my answer and could not come to the realization that 'it' is never two."

Bruce Lee understood the false division that so often traps students of Taoism, the false division in recognizing Yin and Yang as opposites, and not as complements. The Tao is the undivided path.

Lee's fight with Wong Jack Man at his Oakland school brought that fact into deep focus. Fighting strictly in the Wing Chun "style", Lee nearly lost the engagement. By continuing to accept Wing Chun as the solution, Bruce Lee realized he was "clinging to one partial segment of the totality". Lee understood that he must continue to evolve. The idea of styles of fighting came into conflict with his philosophical beliefs that the way of fighting is formless and all-encompassing, and that styles separate the fighter from the truth.

It was at this point that Bruce Lee's expression of martial arts and philosophy, Jeet Kune Do, was born. Its chief principle of "having no way as way" borrowed heavily from Lao Tzu, "This is called shape without shape, form without object."

Bruce Lee student Daniel Lee recognized the influence of Taoism in Bruce Lee's teachings. "To make an art unique, it must have a philosophical foundation. Bruce Lee saw his Jeet Kune Do principles in the Taoist philosophy, the relationship of yin and yang. Jeet Kune Do really is *philosophy in action.*"

Basketball star and Bruce Lee student Kareem Abdul-Jabbar shared a similar view of Bruce and his martial art. "I kind of saw Bruce as a renegade Taoist priest."

Friend and fellow martial artist Leo Fong remembers a conversation he had with Lee in 1964. "Bruce asked me, *'Why are you taking all these gung fu classes?'*

"I said, *'Well, I'm looking for the ultimate.'*

"Bruce let out a big laugh. He said, *'Man, there ain't no ultimate! The ultimate is within you!'*

"It took me a while to let go of the old beliefs, the old crutches. When I got around to letting go and started to train on my own, I realized what Bruce had imparted to me. It's frightening being your own teacher. The only way you can find the cause of your own ignorance, he said, is self-evaluation and total commitment to your own process toward growth."

The second biggest influence on Bruce Lee, philosophically, was the Brahmin philosopher Jiddu Krishnamurti. Krishnamurti was born into poverty in 1895 in southern India. An unusually compassionate and intellectual boy, at the age of 10 he was identified as a mes-

Jiddu Krishnamurti's philosophical ideas eschewing formalized knowledge struck a chord with Bruce Lee.

siah by the mystical Theosophical Society sect. The society convinced Krishnamurti's father to allow the organization to adopt him, and Krishnamurti was sent to Europe to be educated – with the goal that he would eventually assume his role as their leader. However, in 1929, when the time of ascension arrived, Krishnamurti shocked the Theosophical Society by renouncing his role as the messiah, arguing that religious doctrines and organizations were not the path to truth. "Because you have placed beliefs before life, creeds before life, dogmas before life, religions before life, there is stagnation. Can you bind the waters of the sea or gather the winds in your fists?" After renouncing his connection to the Theosophical Society, Krishnamurti became a very influential motivational and philosophical speaker until his death in 1986.

Bruce Lee found that Krishnamurti's viewpoints on life ran parallel to his own. In his book *Freedom from the Known,* Krishnamurti writes: "You cannot look through an ideology, through a screen of words, through hopes and fears. The man who is really serious, with the urge to find out what truth is, has no concept at all. He lives only in what is." Bruce Lee adapted this idea in forming his martial art philosophy: "You cannot express and be alive through static put-together form, through stylized movement. The man who is really serious, with the urge to find out what truth is, has no style at all. He lives only in what is."

Soon Bruce Lee began to study other styles, incorporating what he found useful. He adopted footwork from fencing, for example, and some hand strikes from Western boxing, to name a few. By November 1966, Bruce Lee's new vision for fighting was taking shape. In 1967, he coined the name *Jeet Kune Do* to represent his personal expression of the martial arts. Lee designed a symbol for Jeet Kune Do that consisted of the Tai Chi symbol with two arrows around it moving in opposite directions. This implied the constant interchange between yin and yang.

Bruce Lee defined his Jeet Kune Do thus: "Jeet Kune Do is training and discipline toward the ultimate reality in self-defense, the ultimate reality in simplicity. The true art of Jeet Kune Do is not to accumulate but to eliminate. Totality and freedom of expression toward the ever-changing opponent should be the goal of all practitioners of Jeet Kune Do."

"A classicist or traditionalist will only do what the teacher tells him and that's it. The teacher is pedestalized, you do what he says, and you don't question him," said John Little, the former literary executor of the Bruce Lee Estate. "But Bruce was drawing from some very diverse sources, such as Gestalt therapy, Krishnamurti, etc. Not that these people were necessarily creators either, but they saw a certain truth that they wrote about. Bruce saw that same truth, and he saw its application to martial arts."

"The amazing thing about Bruce was that he was able to bring in things from (what we would think) is outside and make it a part of Jeet Kune Do," recalled Leo Fong.

Bruce Lee's Los Angeles Chinatown student Bob Bremer remembers Lee relating to him the story of the "Chinese Woodcutter":

> "The old Chinese woodcutter was out in the forest chopping wood," said Bruce Lee. "He's chopping the wood and chopping the wood and pretty soon the bushes start rattling and the trees start vibrating. He looks over there, the bushes part and out steps a dragon. The Chinese woodcutter says to himself, *Golly! I always thought they were just stories! This is real! If I could capture it or kill it, I could be famous! I wouldn't have to cut wood anymore!*
>
> "So, he took his ax and takes a step toward the dragon. The dragon turns and says, 'Oh, oh, oh. *You son of a bitch.* I know what you're thinking. If you take another step toward me, I'm going to breathe fire all over you and burn you to a cinder.'
>
> "The woodcutter thinks, He can read my mind! He knows what I'm thinking before I even do it! It's hopeless! I might as well go back to chopping wood!
>
> "So, he goes back to chopping his wood and he's chopping and chopping. In the middle of one of his swings the ax flies out of his hand and hits the dragon right between the eyes. Kills him."

"Bruce never told me what he meant by that story," said Bremer.

"For months I was thinking, *What was he trying to tell me? I'm going over there to learn a physical thing and he's messing with my mind! What the hell is going on?*"

Bruce Lee was trying to instill in his students the natural spontaneity of combat, to reach a point where the action becomes thoughtless, where there is no separation between the fighter and the fight. When there is no intention to act, there can be no expectation of action. This is where the importance of *wu-shin,* or no mindedness comes into play. Also called *mushin* by the Zen masters, wu-shin is the art of detachment, wherein a person learns to let his mind wander free of thought on no particular thing. In this way, the mind can be most efficiently responsive to whatever comes. Like an echo or a reflection in the mirror, the reaction is instantaneous and without conscious thought.

Bruce Lee believed that he could not teach his students so much as point them in the direction of knowledge. "I cannot teach you," Bruce Lee mused to James Franciscus in the television series *Longstreet,* "only help you to explore yourself."

"He actually was one of the very few that applied the philosophy to the art," said Dan Inosanto. "Everything he taught was like *'Be soft, yet not yielding. Firm, yet not hard.'* I was thinking, 'What the hell does that mean?'"

Inosanto was not alone when it came to being confused by

Bruce Lee's philosophical nature. "He often spoke in parables," said author Joe Hyams.

One of Bruce Lee's favorite parables was the story of the Western scholar who came to Japan to learn about Zen from an old Zen master. As the story goes, the two sat down to introductory tea, and it became evident after a few minutes that the Western scholar was more interested in telling the Zen master what he knew than learning anything from him. As the Zen master poured the tea for his guest, the scholar continued to ramble on. The tea began to spill over the edges of the cup; the Zen master continued pouring. "Sir!" said the Western scholar. "The cup is over-full!"

"Yes," replied the Zen master, "and like this cup you, too, are over-filled with your own ideas and opinions. How do you expect to learn if you are not willing to empty your cup?"

Bruce Lee would often quote this parable to his students. He encouraged them to speak up if they had a difference of opinion in his teachings but, if pushed too long, he would say, "At least empty your cup and try." Lee believed that you should not dismiss something out of hand without first investigating it for yourself.

Bruce Lee also felt that knowledge is useless if it is not put to good use. More importantly, one can never determine the value of knowledge if it is not tested. To quote Lao Tzu: "Tao people never try. They do."

Bruce Lee embodied the Taoist concept of *tzu jan,* or honest self-expression. Because he refused to subordinate himself to one style of fighting, he was free to be open and critical of all fighting concepts, including his own. This part of Bruce Lee's character caused the greatest conflict between himself and others, especially martial artists who were trained to accept the teachings of their instructor without question. Indeed, the term *master,* used in many martial arts styles to denote the teacher or leader of the school, implies absolute and unquestioning authority. As the ancient Greek philosopher Socrates first explained, the best path to knowledge and wisdom is through the *dialectic,* or the process of placing ideas in open discussion so that the inherent weaknesses of the ideas can be discovered. This Socratic Method is now used, not only in philosophy, but also in the scientific method of examination, wherein a researcher will first formulate a hypothesis and then try to prove or disprove it. The science of martial arts should be no different.

Bruce Lee's personal expression of martial arts was something that he believed was unique to him and him alone, because it was the product of his personal attributes and deficiencies. Among his physical "quirks" were poor eyesight, being short and lightweight, a bad back, and one leg that was shorter than the other. What he lacked in these areas he made up for in speed, timing, and strength. Dan Inosanto, the instructor at his Los Angeles school, said, "The total picture Bruce Lee wanted to present to his pupil was that, above everything else, he must find his own way. It is important to remember that Bruce Lee was a 'pointer' to the truth and not the truth itself."

Bruce Lee did not believe in learning by accumulation, but instead believed that the highest form of mastery was one of simplicity, of *stripping away the inessentials,* much like Lao Tzu believed in the need to disband all schools of formal learning. Indeed, Lee disbanded his own school system shortly before his death, lest his way be taken as "the way".

For Bruce Lee, all knowledge led to self-knowledge. Lee placed a great deal of emphasis on this belief in his teachings. It was one of the most important concepts he derived from his study of Krishnamurti. As Krishnamurti said: "We must first understand ourselves in order to know anything and to understand and solve problems." Lee felt that, for a person to grow and evolve, they must come to know themselves through whatever medium they choose: dance, music, art, or martial arts to name a few.

Clearly, Bruce Lee was most influenced by the Taoist theories of Lao Tzu. As Diane Dreher wrote in her book *The Tao of Inner Peace,* "Unlike Confucius, who upheld tradition, Lao Tzu appeals to progressive individuals who think for themselves, depart from convention, and seek the higher truth. He knew that new solutions rarely come from old leaders, entrenched in the status quo. Often, they come from ordinary people who believe in the power to make a difference."

Perhaps in the end it will be the philosophy of Bruce Lee that has the greatest importance in a historical perspective. Lee has influenced generations since his passing with his concepts of liberation from classical thought, bending to adversity, economy of action, and openness to learn. These are concepts that will greatly benefit people of all doctrines, disciplines, and vocations.

BRUCE LEE: MOVIE STAR

There are two ways of making a good living. One is the result of hard working, and the other, the result of the imagination (requires work, too, of course).

Bruce Lee

Bruce Lee was destined to be a movie star. It was in his blood. His father was a career entertainer, appearing on stage and in countless Hong Kong movies. Lee himself did some 20 movies as a child. With his grace, athleticism, extroverted personality, and flair for dramatics, it was no surprise that American filmmakers discovered him. The question was timing.

Bruce Lee's big break came at Ed Parker's 1964 Long Beach Tournament. It was there that hairstylist-to-the-stars Jay Sebring (who would later become one of the murder victims of the infamous Manson Family along with Lee's friend, actress Sharon Tate) saw Lee's impressive martial arts demonstration. Shortly thereafter, Sebring told one of his clients, *Batman* TV producer William Dozier, about Bruce Lee. Dozier was looking for a handsome young Asian man to play the title role in a Charlie Chan inspired series called *Number One Son*. He thought Lee might be his man.

After viewing the film footage Ed Parker shot of Bruce Lee at the tournament, Dozier arranged a screen test for Lee. He did well in the screen test, though the concept for the series was not sold. Not to matter, because Dozier had another series in the works called *The Green Hornet*. Designed to be a companion show for his then new *Batman* series, Dozier wanted Bruce Lee for the title character's Asian manservant Kato. He would be the Green Hornet's "Robin", so to speak, though in reality he was more of a "Tonto".

The series commenced filming in June of 1966. Immediately, there was a problem with filming. In the fight scenes, Bruce Lee was moving so fast that the camera was not picking it up! Lee had to slow down his movements and the cameraman had to over-crank (shoot more frames per second) to catch the action. It was also at this point that Bruce Lee suggested they show the footage in slow motion, a practice that has become the standard for martial arts movies and television shows.

The first show appeared on ABC on Friday, September 9, 1966. Though the character of Kato was supposed to be the sidekick of the lead character Green Hornet, Bruce Lee's martial arts expertise and on-screen intensity usually outshone Green Hornet actor Van Williams' John Wayne-style Hollywood fisticuffs. For most TV viewers, this was their first exposure to kung fu, and they were mesmerized by what they saw. The producers were not comfortable at all with the co-star outshining the star, and this led to continual efforts by the powers-that-be to "reign in" Bruce Lee.

Both stars began making public appearances to promote the show, including radio and television appearances. Lee especially worked the public, giving martial arts demonstrations at fairs, public parks, and martial arts tournaments.

To help boost the ratings of *The Green Hornet,* a crossover episode with the *Batman* series was arranged. The episode called for the obligatory fight between the two teams, and it was decided that, since *Batman* was the more popular series, that the Green Hornet and Kato would lose to the Batman and Robin, respectively.

When Bruce Lee read the script for the episode, he became incensed. There was no way his character was going to lose to that silly *Biff! Bam! Pow!* boy in the pantyhose. Lee let his displeasure about the situation be known to the producers in a very vocal way, arguing that the viewers would not buy it. It was instead decided that the fight would be a draw.

Stuntman Victor Paul remembered filming the fight scene. "We had quite an incident, because Batman and Robin didn't want to

Bruce Lee and Van Williams in the Green Hornet *(20th Century Fox)*

lose the fight. Bruce Lee didn't want to lose the fight either. They had a big to-do about that. Bruce Lee said, *'Nobody beats me.'* Finally, we had to get the producer to come down and straighten out the whole deal. We just sat there and waited. He said, *'Look, it's a Mexican standoff. Nobody wins. You have this big fight. At the end of it, you just stop it and stare at each other; that's the end of the fight.'* So that's how we did it."

Since Paul was the stunt double for Robin actor Burt Ward, he was worried about the aggressive Bruce Lee, with whom he would have to work. "I talked to Bruce Lee," said Paul. "I said, *'Bruce, whatever you do, don't nail me, because I'll come back with a chair on you.'* He was fast; if he hit you, he'd knock your head off and he was used to making contact. I said, *'Don't make any contact with me because that's not right.'*"

During the period when Bruce Lee was openly voicing his opposition to the scene, actor Burt Ward was running his mouth off, too, telling the production staff that he was a black belt and could hold his own against Lee. In truth, there was only one martial artist working for William Dozier at the time and that was Bruce Lee. When word got back to him about Burt Ward's comments, Lee put the word out: he was going to pulverize Robin for real when they filmed the fight scene. The effect was that Burt Ward was terrified of the coming fight. Adam West (Batman) told Van Williams that "Burt Ward was pissing in his pants!"

When it came time for the scene, Bruce Lee didn't speak a word; he just glared at Burt Ward. When the director yelled action, Lee started following Ward around the room and Ward began running for his life, breaking out of character screaming, "It's only a TV show!"

Bruce Lee chased after him until he was cornered, at which point Lee, the cast, and the crew broke into laughter.

"You're lucky it is a TV show," said Bruce Lee.

Despite the best efforts of those involved, *The Green Hornet* failed to catch on with the general public and was canceled on July 14, 1967, after only 26 episodes. Producer William Dozier notified Bruce Lee of the cancellation with the patently racist note: *"Confucius say, Green Hornet to buzz no more."*

The period after *The Green Hornet* cancellation was a financially troubling one for Bruce Lee and his family. Lee focused his attention on teaching while he tried to develop a new show with producer Fred Wientraub. As conceived by Bruce Lee, the show was going to be called *The Warrior* and would feature a renegade Chinese warrior in the Old West.

While *The Warrior* was in development, Bruce Lee kept afloat by guest starring in episodes of *Ironside, Blondie,* and *Here Comes the Brides*. He also worked as a fight coordinator for the movies *The Wrecking Crew* and *A Walk in the Spring Rain*. In the 1969 movie *Marlowe,* Bruce Lee had a memorable cameo where he walked into star James Garner's office and destroyed it with his bare hands. In addition, Lee made money charging his celebrity students up to $250 an hour for instruction.

These temporary jobs helped pay the bills while Bruce Lee waited for word on *The Warrior*. Eventually, he would be notified that *The Warrior* was not moving forward. Instead, a competing series proposal, with a very similar concept, *Kung Fu,* was greenlit. They gave its lead role to a Caucasian actor, David Carradine, who knew nothing about the martial arts. Although he would have been perfect for the job, the producers passed on casting Bruce Lee for the lead because they thought he looked too "Chinese" and were afraid American audiences would not accept him.

Bruce Lee was extremely disappointed and hurt by Hollywood's racism. While he struggled to find opportunities in America, a visit to Hong Kong made it apparent that Lee was not unappreciated everywhere. Since the cancellation of *The Green Hornet,* the series was broadcast in Hong Kong, where it caused quite a sensation.

Bruce Lee arrived in Hong Kong to find that he was a celebrity. Using that momentum, he approached Run Run Shaw, head of the Shaw Brothers film company, to offer his services. Run Run Shaw offered Lee a seven-year contract and US $75 a week which, though laughable, was a good deal better than the US $10 a week that Shaw's regular actors were making. Bruce Lee laughed at the offer and turned it down. He returned to America.

Bruce Lee teaching James Franciscus Jeet Kune Do in the television series Longstreet (Paramount)

Back in America, Bruce Lee's student Stirling Siliphant was developing a new television series entitled *Longstreet*, about a blind police detective. He wrote a part for Lee in the premiere episode that would spotlight his teacher. The title of the first episode was "Way of the Intercepting Fist" – the literal translation of Jeet Kune Do. Bruce Lee played a character that was essentially himself, and he even co-wrote his own dialogue with Siliphant. In the episode, his character taught Jeet Kune Do to the blind detective. Bruce Lee's appearance was the only saving grace of the show and, just like *The Green Hornet,* Lee was getting more fan mail than the star.

Shortly before the *Longstreet* premiere was filmed, Bruce Lee received a call from Raymond Chow with Golden Harvest Studio in Hong Kong. Golden Harvest was a small independent film studio struggling to get out of the shadow of rival Shaw Brothers. Chow offered Lee US $15,000 for two pictures. Before he made a decision, Bruce Lee watched all the movies put out by Golden Harvest to date. He was disappointed with what he saw. Everybody fought the same, and there was little in the way of plot or motivation, just continual, mindless violence. When he next talked to Raymond Chow he asked him frankly, "Is this the best you can do?" Chow said yes. Bruce Lee told him he could do better, and that he would show him how.

In July 1971, Bruce Lee made the trip to Thailand to film *The Big Boss,* the first of his two-picture deal with Golden Harvest. When he arrived in the tiny village of Pak Chong, he met with Raymond Chow. Bruce Lee shook his hand and said, "You just wait, I'm going to be the biggest Chinese star in the world."

The working and living conditions in Pak Chong were atrocious. The area was infested with mosquitoes, cockroaches, and lizards. The heat was intolerable, and the food was almost inedible – what there was of it.

The filming was especially demanding on Bruce Lee. At one point, he received a serious cut on his hand that required 10 stitches. A previous back injury was a constant source of pain and irritation. Working past the point of exhaustion, Lee lost 10 pounds. He caught the flu. Lastly, Bruce Lee sprained his ankle and had to finish the fight scenes dragging his leg.

While Bruce Lee was suffering in Thailand, the success of his *Longstreet* appearance allowed him to negotiate a few more episodes. Lee would eventually do four episodes for the series.

The Big Boss premiered in Hong Kong in October of 1971. Bruce Lee was very nervous about the premiere; Hong Kong audiences could be very unforgiving if they did not like a movie. They were known to jeer and even cause property damage.

At the conclusion of the film, the audience was absolutely silent. The credits rolled and not a word was uttered. No one moved. Bruce Lee was sure his movie was a bomb. Then, as the credits ended, the theater exploded in applause. The attendees were so impressed by the movie that they first took note of every name involved with the production and then, only at the end of the credits, did they voice their appreciation for the film and its star, Bruce Lee.

Within 19 days the movie made $3.5 million dollars, breaking the Hong Kong box office record previously held by *The Sound of Music* at $2.3 million. It went on to break records throughout Asia.

It was official: Bruce Lee was a *star,* if in Asia only. Though he wanted the brass ring, namely American celebrity, he would settle with Asian stardom for the moment. What mattered was that Bruce

Bruce Lee strikes a blow against racism. (Alamy)

Lee was now being recognized for his efforts and appreciated.

Shaw Brothers CEO Run Run Shaw took notice of Bruce Lee's newfound success. Lee managed to help Golden Harvest become a contender in the Hong Kong filmmaking scene, and that jeopardized Shaw Brothers' position. To change that, Run Run Shaw approached Lee with a *new offer*. Just months prior, Shaw offered Bruce Lee a mere $75 a week. Now he offered him $248,000. When Lee turned it down, Shaw sent him a blank check and told him to put whatever number on it he felt he was worth. Again, Bruce Lee turned him down. Lee gave his word to Golden Harvest, and he intended to honor that.

Bruce Lee went right into his next production for Golden Harvest Studios. *Fist of Fury* was loosely based on the murder of Sifu Ho Yuan Chia, a kung fu instructor who was killed by members of a competing Japanese karate school in 1908. Lee played the part of Chen Chen, a student of Sifu Ho's who seeks revenge for the murder of his teacher. The movie plays off the Chinese dislike of the Japanese, who occupied China during the period in which the move takes place. Bruce Lee's character becomes a wanted man as he methodically picks off his teacher's killers. In the climax of the movie, Lee squares off with the master of the Japanese school and kills him. The movie ends with Bruce Lee's character jumping toward a crowd of police who open fire on him.

The movie was made in six weeks, though, to Bruce Lee, it seemed much longer. Lo Wei, the director of *The Big Boss,* was again the director for *Fist of Fury,* despite the fact that Lee developed an open dislike for Wei's nonchalant attitude about filmmaking. Bruce Lee was accustomed to a Hollywood production, and he was bothered by the Hong Kong process of filming movies without a script – making it up as they went along. Lee was determined to put out the best product he could. "I have to say that cinema is a marriage of art and business," Bruce Lee said. "The actor is not a human being but a product, a commodity. However, as a human being, I have the right to be the best goddamn product that ever walked and work so hard that the business people have to listen to you." Lo Wei, on the other hand, refused to listen to Bruce Lee's suggestions for improving production and felt that Lee had a lot of nerve to tell the veteran director how to do his job.

The two creators managed to complete the movie despite their differences. When *Fist of Fury* was released, it was an even bigger success than *The Big Boss*. The Chinese audiences went crazy when Lee defended his people, soundly trouncing the Japanese and declaring, "The Chinese are not the sick people of Asia!" Now Bruce Lee was not just a celebrity, he was a *megastar*.

Bruce Lee completed his two-picture deal with Golden Harvest and was free to negotiate a new contract. He was also receiving offers from outside Hong Kong. Producers in Italy and Hungary were pursuing Lee to make pictures for them. MGM even contacted Bruce Lee about making a movie with Elvis Presley, who was a student of Kenpo under Lee's friend, Ed Parker.

Bruce Lee instead approached Raymond Chow about a new deal: a partnership in which he and Chow would be equals. Though Chow disliked the idea of giving up his control, he knew that Lee could now write his own ticket, and that ticket might well take him to Run Run Shaw's door. Their new company, Concord Productions, was born.

Bruce Lee exercised his new-found authority by refusing to work with Lo Wei on his next picture, publicly saying, "No way, Lo Wei!" Lee decided he would direct his next picture, which he would write as well. The film would be called *Way of the Dragon*. Lee's professional move was shocking to the movie community in Hong Kong. Until that time, actors in Hong Kong had no input into the cinematic product other than to perform and take home their $10. Now Bruce Lee, on the strength of two pictures, changed everything. The result was that other actors and production employees began to receive a bigger piece of the pie. Lee had given his colleagues the means, and the courage, to demand better for themselves.

Meanwhile, Lo Wei was upset that his new meal ticket washed his hands of Wei. He publicly criticized Bruce Lee, told a reporter that, "Bruce does not understand fighting for the camera," called him an unaccomplished streetfighter, and said that he had to teach Bruce Lee "how to fight for movies". This led to further animosity between the two.

Bruce Lee forged ahead with *Way of the Dragon*. He decided to film in Rome, the first time that a Chinese picture would ever be made outside of China. The movie was a labor of love for Lee, and he put his heart and soul into it. Lee again played the archetypal Chinese small-town boy, which was the favored character for Chinese audiences. His character comes to Rome to defend a Chinese restaurant against the Caucasian mafia. Chinese audiences enjoyed seeing their hero beat up Japanese and Caucasians, and Bruce Lee took the opportunity to showcase his student Chuck Norris in the film. Norris brought along fellow martial artist Bob Wall, who was previously "uninvited" to the production by Bruce Lee. Wall was a close friend of Norris and a student of Joe Lewis, but he was also someone whom Lee knew in California and would rather forget. However, since Bob Wall was already there, Lee went ahead and utilized him in the film. Regardless of personal conflicts, Lee rightly believed that having real martial artists perform the fight scenes added authenticity to the production.

The movie was filmed clandestinely around Rome. After Lee was refused a permit, parts of the final fight scene between Bruce Lee and Chuck Norris was shot in the Roman Colosseum without permission. The interior shots were filmed back in Hong Kong, where Bruce Lee used his own cat in the film as the sole witness of the Colosseum fight.

When Bruce Lee returned to Hong Kong, he told reporters emphatically that *"The Way of the Dragon* will gross over five million dollars in Hong Kong alone." The press laughed at him. They stopped laughing when the picture brought in $5.4 million in its first three weeks.

"What set the Bruce Lee movies apart, clearly, was Bruce Lee," said writer Alex Ben Block, who interviewed Lee shortly before his death. "When you sat in the theater he was right there in your face. There are very few actors who can achieve that. There was a sincerity and intensity that was so amazing that it was undeniable. It made little kids jump on the top of their seats and start screaming; it made women swoon; it made men excited that here was an action hero that they could identify with."

Bruce Lee immediately began work on his fourth feature, *Game of Death*. It was planned as the ultimate martial arts movie. In the movie, Lee's character was to enter a pagoda wherein he would face a different opponent on each level, each more difficult than the last. Among the martial artists Bruce Lee brought in for the fight scenes were his students Kareem Abdul-Jabbar and Dan Inosanto. The fight scene with Kareem Abdul-Jabbar was especially interesting to see, as the 7' 2" Kareem Abdul-Jabbar towered over Bruce Lee.

The fight scene with Dan Inosanto featured a classic battle with nunchaku. It was Inosanto who introduced Lee to the Okinawan weapon. Said Inosanto: "He thought it was a flashy, worthless piece of shit! But he felt it was very effective for the movies. Sifu Bruce can be very blunt."

Bruce Lee filmed about a half hour of useable footage for *Game of Death* before he received a call from Fred Weintraub, the Hollywood producer with whom he once planned to make *The Warrior* television series. The executives in Hollywood were monitoring the box office receipts Lee was generating in Asia. Money talks, and they were ready to make a Bruce Lee movie. A hasty deal was put together and *Enter the Dragon* went into production. *Game of Death* was halted temporarily while Lee completed the American film.

Despite the fact that his previous movies were a big hit in Asia, Bruce Lee was worried if American audiences would accept him. As the time to start shooting the picture came close, Lee grew even more nervous and failed to show up on set. He kept making excuses for why he could not perform. In turn, the producers were getting worried. For two weeks in January 1973, they had to shoot scenes around his character, waiting for Bruce Lee to appear. Finally, Lee's wife, Linda, persuaded him to begin filming. That first day, Bruce Lee was so nervous that the production managed to film only one shot of him, the shot in which he catches a piece of fruit that was hit by a dart. After that, Bruce Lee eased into the production and overcame his nervousness.

The production of *Enter the Dragon* was not easy for its participants, especially Bruce Lee. There were the obvious physical demands: Lee would have to film scenes where he fought against 10

Bruce Lee called the nunchaku "a flashy, worthless, piece of shit" that was impractical for real combat, but he nonetheless felt that they made for good cinema. (Alamy)

to 20 men, sometimes in 15 or 20 takes. He also dealt with the racism of the American production team. At one point, Robert Clouse, the director, was mad at Lee and passive-aggressively needled him by changing the name of a Caucasian character Lee had a scene with to *Braithwaite,* a name he knew Bruce Lee would have difficulty pronouncing.

One of the biggest nuisances for Bruce Lee on the set of *Enter the Dragon* was the constant challenges from Chinese extras hired to fill out the background scenes. Many of these extras were cocky Triads, a network of organized gangs in China and Hong Kong. Triads are similar in function and organization to the American mafia. These young men wanted to make a name for themselves by taking on the great Bruce Lee. They would announce their challenge to Lee by approaching him, folding their arms, and stomping their feet three times. This was shocking behavior to the American crew, who had never seen such a scenario in their lives, but to Bruce Lee it was a common occurrence, no different than the gunslingers of the Old West challenging each other to see who was the fastest draw.

"The situation on a film set is a little different," said Linda Lee

Cadwell, Bruce Lee's widow. "Here you have someone (Bruce) who really can do what he says he can do. He's not just an actor; he's not just a stuntman. He really can fight. But at the same time, they have to stage these fights, choreograph them, so that no one gets hurt. You have to maintain the confidence of all of these extras that you are a man who really knows what you can do without actually getting into fights. So, there was a constant balance that Bruce had to maintain."

For the most part, Bruce Lee ignored these challenges, but on a couple of occasions the challengers hit a nerve with Lee. "Bruce felt that the goading got to the point where, if he didn't do something, the group would get behind it and he (Bruce) would be lacking in credibility. He needed all these people to work with him in choreographing these huge fights, so they had to be with him in the spirit of it and not just thinking, *'He's just a paper tiger'*," notes Cadwell.

In one instance, Bruce Lee called his challenger to come down to him. He told the man to "show me what you know" and then tied the man up with his trapping skills and put him on the ground. The crowd cheered their approval of Lee, and he sent the challenger back to his place on the wall.

"The way that Bruce handled the situation was that he created the perfect balance, because then he had all the stuntmen working with him without ever having hurt anybody, without having thrown this person out and humiliating him," said Cadwell. "This guy was now on his side, so this was an efficient technique for what he wanted to accomplish."

Bruce Lee historian John Little makes another interesting point about the incident. "It's interesting that Bruce could have had license to do something: he could have fired him off the set or he could have sent him to the hospital. Instead, he just sent him back up on the wall. *And he corrected his form.*"

Another challenge Bruce Lee accepted may not have been on one of Lee's more charitable days. Looking him in the eye, Lee asked the man what he knew about Jeet Kune Do. "I know enough," the man replied. The man threw a kick at Bruce Lee; he did not react to it, knowing it would fall short. Then Lee took the offensive, erupting with three rapid-fire shots. The man appeared unmarked by Bruce Lee's attack until he opened his mouth and blood spilled out onto the ground.

Bruce Lee would play around with the extras and the technicians on the set, often challenging them in games of skill. One

While filming Enter the Dragon, *Bruce Lee had to deal with constant challenges to his reputation as the king of the martial arts.* (Globe Photos)

of the more dangerous games Lee liked to play was with a meat cleaver and a peanut. Lee would ask the other person to try to chop his fingers off before he could pick the peanut up off the chopping board. Bruce Lee never lost.

The outside tournament scenes were filmed on a Hong Kong lawyer's estate. It was built next to a relatively undeveloped area. The extras from the movie would often wander out into those woods to follow the trails and nap under trees. On one of their excursions, they found the corpse of a young woman. The filming of the movie had to be suspended until the police were able to determine that no one involved in the production committed the murder.

The most talked about occurrence during the filming of *Enter the Dragon* was the "accidental" cutting of Bruce Lee by actor Bob Wall. Wall was playing the hired henchman of the movie's villain. He had previously been in Lee's last movie, *Way of the Dragon*, the one to which he was "uninvited". In *Enter the Dragon*, the producers needed a martial artist who could play a real son-of-a-bitch, and Bruce Lee knew Bob Wall fit the bill.

The scene called for Bruce Lee's character and Wall's character to face off in a tournament competition. Bruce Lee's character, Lee, was supposed to get the upper hand, forcing a desperate and dishonorable Ohara (Wall) to pick up a bottle, break it, and go after Bruce Lee with it. Lee would then kick the bottle out of his hand and deliver the *coup de grâce*.

The scene was choreographed, and the actors took their places. Wall's job called for him to release the bottle when Bruce Lee executed the kick that was supposed to "knock" the bottle out of Wall's hand. When Lee performed the kick and spun around, Wall ignored his cue to drop the jagged bottle which, being real glass, cut Lee's hand open when Wall grazed it on his follow through.

The cut was deep and debilitating, resulting in 12 stitches. Bruce Lee was unable to film for a week. Rumors began to spread that Bob Wall intentionally held on to the bottle to screw with Lee. Bruce Lee believed the same thing and decided that, when filming resumed (which involved finishing the fight scene with Wall), he would make his displeasure known. "That dumb Bob Wall," Bruce Lee said. "I told him that I was going to kick a broken bottle out of his hand, and we practiced it several times. But when they started shooting, I kicked his hand, but instead of letting the bottle go, he hung on to it."

Bruce Lee told some of the stuntmen of his intentions to kill Bob Wall, who in turn told the director. The director went to Lee and begged him not to kill Wall. Bruce Lee was adamant that Wall was going to get his due. Finally, director Robert Clouse lied to him, saying that Wall was needed for some shots in the United States and that, if Lee killed him, the film could not be completed. Bruce Lee reluctantly agreed to tone down his response.

Wall, for his part, heard the rumors of Bruce Lee's intentions and was sweating bullets. Later, years after Lee's death, Wall would turn bad-mouthing Bruce Lee into a semi-career, telling people that Lee was not a good fighter and that he had no sense of timing. But, at that moment, Bob Wall was honestly worried about his safety and well-being.

Bruce Lee returned to filming and, on the first day back, he and Bob Wall were scheduled to finish their fight scene together. The final shot filmed required Lee to sidekick Wall. This shot actually precedes the shot in which Bruce Lee was injured in the movie. In preparation for this stunt, Bob Wall wore a chest pad to ensure his safety. Several takes of the scene were shot. Each time, Bruce

Bob Wall earned the wrath of Bruce Lee on the set of Enter the Dragon. (Warner Brothers)

Lee's kicks were "off", hitting Wall everywhere but on the padding, kind of strange for a man who did not miss. After each take, Lee would turn to his stuntmen and ask them (in Cantonese) if Wall had been punished enough. They would laugh. Finally, Bruce Lee needed to finish the scene. The cameras rolled and Lee executed the sidekick, knocking Wall back so hard he flew into the crowd behind him, breaking the arm of one of the extras on impact. "Bob went flying," remembers Paul Heller, a producer on *Enter the Dragon*. "He must have gone 30 feet through the chairs, *through everything*. And he was going to try to stonewall it – I mean, he was going to just be there and stop Bruce dead!" Though Bruce Lee did not kill Wall, he definitely made his point.

In the scene where Bruce Lee enters Han's dungeon, he must overcome a cobra positioned at the door. In the movie, Lee catches the cobra and places it in a bag, to be utilized later. The filming of that scene did not go without incident. Bruce Lee was actually bitten by the cobra, which (fortunately for Lee) was de-venomized. "The damn thing fell asleep on me," said Bruce Lee, "so I tried to wake it up by slapping its head, and instead got bitten on my hand." It should be noted that the cobra was the only opponent of Bruce Lee's that ever beat him to the punch!

Bruce Lee on the set of Enter the Dragon *contemplating a bad decision.* (Globe Photos)

As a matter of trivia, the group fight scene against Bruce Lee in the dungeon included a young extra named Jackie Chan, who would go on to take up the mantle of martial arts movie master after Bruce Lee's death.

The climactic fight scene between Han and Bruce Lee required both actors to trade flying sidekicks with each other. The director was not satisfied with the shot and kept reshooting it. Shot after shot took its toll on Lee, and he received a serious groin injury that stopped filming for a few weeks.

The fight scene at the end of *Enter the Dragon*, in which all the extras fight each other on the tournament field in a free-for-all, actually turned into a real fight when the Triads from competing gangs tried to kill each other.

The last scene filmed for *Enter the Dragon* was the first scene seen chronologically. It was the scene in which Bruce Lee takes on the Shaolin monk in a challenge match that opens the movie. Lee added the scene because he felt the opening needed a little more "punch". His opponent in this scene was played by Sammo Hung, who would go on to make a name for himself as an actor and director of Hong Kong martial arts movies.

On July 20, 1973, Bruce Lee died in the apartment of Hong Kong film actress Betty Ting Pei. The circumstances of his death have remained unclear, partly due to the efforts of Bruce Lee's business partner, Raymond Chow, and Lee's wife, Linda, to avoid the public revelation that Bruce Lee died in the apartment of a woman who was not his wife. Despite their efforts, this bit of information quickly became known.

While the Asian world was reeling from the death of Bruce Lee, Lee's business partner Raymond Chow was looking for a way to make a quick buck off his dead cash cow. Chow hurriedly cobbled together a documentary about the life of Bruce Lee, entitled *Bruce Lee: The Man and the Legend,* which was released in Hong Kong on September 4, 1973. The exploitive film was released a mere two weeks after his death and even included tasteless footage of Bruce Lee's corpse in his casket.

Three weeks after Bruce Lee died, *Enter the Dragon* was released in the United States and became an immediate hit. The movie, made for around $800,000, made $3 million in its first seven weeks alone. Its success spread to Europe and then worldwide. It would eventually make over $200 million, making it one of the most profitable movies of all time.

The world was now clamoring for more Bruce Lee, and people were doing everything they could to fill the void. MGM re-released the movie *Marlowe*, giving Bruce Lee's bit part top billing over star James Garner. Twentieth Century Fox packaged some episodes of *The Green Hornet* together and sold it as a movie. In Hong Kong, the movie studios began cranking out bad Bruce Lee imitators: Bruce Li, Bruce Le, Bruce Leong, and Bruce Rhe, to name just a

It was not until Jackie Chan developed his own unique brand of cinema fighting that the martial arts movie genre flourished again. (Photo courtesy of Dith Hat)

few. Some of the silliest were the ones that adopted the names of western action stars, such as Clint (Eastwood?) Lee and (Charles?) Bronson Lee. They were always the next big thing, the "next Bruce Lee". It was not until Jackie Chan developed his unique approach to martial arts movies (that was not a pale imitation of Bruce Lee) that the genre flourished again.

In 1978, Raymond Chow released *Game of Death*. Instead of packaging the 15 minutes of original fight footage of Bruce Lee with a tasteful documentary, Chow hired *Enter the Dragon* director Robert Clouse to mix the original footage with shots of Lee from previous movies and new scenes shot with look-alikes. They even re-used the objectionable footage of Bruce Lee in his own casket as a movie plot point and post-mortem performance. The result was an unintentionally laughable farce that was a financial success despite its poor quality.

It is a testament to Bruce Lee that his movies continue to make money today on video and streaming as new generations are exposed to his talent and genius. Though there have been many who have tried, no one has ever replaced Bruce Lee as the greatest martial arts movie star who ever lived.

BRUCE LEE: FAMILY MAN

The happiness we have today is built on the ordinary life we had before we married. The happiness that is got from ordinary life can last longer: like coal, it burns gradually and slowly. The happiness got from excitement is like a brilliant fire--soon it will go out.

Bruce Lee

Bruce Lee first met Linda Emery at Seattle's Garfield High School in 1963. She was a senior at the high school and Lee was a guest speaker on Chinese philosophy. Soon after, she joined the gung fu class that Lee taught on the campus of the University of Washington. One day, Emery was practicing gung fu with Bruce Lee on campus when Lee asked her if she wanted to go to dinner at the Space Needle, one of Seattle's finest landmarks.

"You mean all of us?" Linda Emery asked, thinking Bruce Lee meant the whole gung fu class.

"No, only you and me," replied Lee.

Bruce Lee liked Linda Emery because she seemed to understand him. They began seeing each other on a regular basis. With Linda's support, Lee opened a gung fu school close to the university campus.

Bruce Lee and Linda Emery grew close over the months. Then

in Spring of 1964, Emery became pregnant. The couple discussed marriage. Although his Seattle gung fu school was making enough money to support Bruce Lee, it would not support a family. Lee believed he would have to be more financially stable before he could care for a wife and child.

Bruce Lee decided his fortunes would be better in California, so he moved to the city of Oakland in June of 1964 with plans to open a second school. As Linda Emery said goodbye to Bruce Lee at the airport, he told her, "I'll be back." Emery was worried that he never would.

Throughout the summer, Bruce Lee and Linda Emery communicated through letters. Because her mother was against interracial dating and they were hiding their relationship, Emery rented a post office box to receive her mail from Lee.

Eventually, Bruce Lee returned to Seattle where he and Linda Emery planned to elope. The couple avoided mentioning their plans to her family, who had never met Lee. On August 12, 1964, the couple went to the King County Courthouse and applied for a marriage license. Unknown to them, applications for marriage are announced in the paper as a matter of public record, and word of the impending nuptials made it back to her mother. Linda Emery's mother asked her daughter to bring Lee to their home, and she had the entire Emery family assembled to help talk them out of marriage.

Their strong-arm tactics did not put off Bruce Lee. When he met Linda Emery's family, Lee told them, tersely, "I want to marry your daughter. By the way, I'm Chinese." Her family attempted to talk them out of it, saying that it would not be a proper Christian marriage and Emery could not cook or take care of the house.

"She'll learn," replied Bruce Lee.

It was not only Bruce Lee's race that worried the Emery family. Lee's finances were meager, and the Emery family did not see how gung fu could make a man a living. They were set against the marriage, and no assurances from Bruce Lee could dissuade them.

Then Bruce Lee and Linda Emery informed her family that she was pregnant.

On August 17, 1964, Bruce Lee and Linda Emery were married at the Seattle Congregational Church. The guests were few. After the wedding, Bruce and Linda Lee moved to Oakland, where they would live with Lee's friend and student James Lee and his wife.

In Oakland, Bruce Lee's new school was not doing so well. To make matters worse, James Lee's wife died unexpectedly of cancer

"Linda and I aren't one and one," said Bruce Lee. "We are two that make a whole. You have to apply yourself to be a family. (Doris Nieh/Globe Photos)

and Linda Lee was thrust into the role of mother and caregiver to James Lee's children, Karena and Greglon. Then Linda Lee gave birth to her own child, Brandon, on February 1, 1965.

A week after Brandon Lee was born, Bruce Lee's father died in Hong Kong. Lee was devastated, despite the fact that father and son were not especially close. Bruce Lee went to Hong Kong for the funeral. While there, he came to terms with his strained relationship with his father. Lee contented himself in the knowledge that his father was happy about the birth of his first grandchild.

At the same time, Bruce Lee was beginning his evolution as a martial artist that would eventually lead him to the creation of Jeet Kune Do. Lee constantly trained, revising his concepts and forging his body. A screen test for 20th Century Fox did not result in a television series as hoped, but Bruce Lee received $1,800 as a retainer for a future project producer William Dozier was planning. Lee used the $1,800 to fly his family to Hong Kong, where they lived for a time.

Hong Kong was especially difficult for Linda Lee. Whereas Bruce Lee had no problem fitting in in America, Linda Lee knew no Cantonese and had to deal with the Lee family's lack of enthusiasm for her. Said Linda: "They would have preferred that Bruce had married a Chinese girl."

After four months in Hong Kong, Bruce and Linda Lee returned to the United States where they stayed with Linda Lee's mother for another four months. Though he continued to teach at his Seattle school (which was run in his absence by student Taky Kimura), Linda's mother always questioned when Lee was going to get a "real job". The Lee family eventually returned to live with James Lee in Oakland.

As soon as they returned to Oakland, Bruce Lee was informed that *The Green Hornet* television series was greenlit. To prepare for the new job, Bruce and Linda Lee rented a house in Los Angeles.

With *The Green Hornet* now in production, Lee was finally making a decent living. To reflect their new "affluence", the family moved to an apartment on Wilshire Boulevard in Westwood and bought a new car.

Unfortunately, *The Green Hornet* lasted only one season and the family again found themselves in financial straits. Bruce Lee used his contacts in Hollywood to teach private lessons to celebrities. The extra income helped a bit.

Lee enjoyed spending time with his wife and son. He especially liked teaching his son gung fu, and they would often play together in the backyard. In 1972, at the age of seven, Brandon appeared with his father on a Hong Kong charity telethon and broke two boards with a sidekick.

"I remember him bringing Brandon over when he could barely crawl," said Fred Sato, a football coach, history teacher, and friend to Bruce Lee. "I knew he had a lot of pride in Brandon. He'd roll a ball to him, and he (Brandon) would kind of push it back and Bruce would say, *'Did you see that!'* and I would say, *'That's fantastic.'* He was a proud father."

Brandon Lee was neither completely Chinese nor American, but Bruce Lee was unconcerned with the potential troubles he would face as a child of mixed-race. Just the opposite, Lee felt that Brandon's heritage would be a source of strength.

"Brandon will learn that Oriental culture and Occidental culture are not mutually exclusive, but mutually dependent," said Bruce Lee. "Neither would be remarkable if it were not for the existence of the other."

The Lee family grew. Bruce and Linda Lee's daughter Shannon was born on April 19, 1969. Bruce Lee was hoping for another boy (the Chinese have a definite preference for male children), but he was pleasantly surprised by the addition of a daughter.

Bruce Lee's son Brandon grew up under the shadow of his famous father but carved out his own legacy as an actor. (Doris Nieh/Globe Photos)

Having Bruce Lee as a father was not an easy experience for his children. While it was great having a dad who had a reputation as one of the country's top martial artists, none of Brandon Lee's friends would come to his house and play because there was always a group of men in his backyard yelling and hitting each other.

Bruce Lee was very concerned about being a capable father to his children. He even read books on child-raising in the hopes that it would make him a better parent. His own father was not the most involved parent, and Lee wanted to make sure that his children got the best father he could give them.

Of marriage, Bruce Lee said: "Marriage is a friendship, a partnership based solidly upon ordinary, everyday occurrences. Marriage is breakfast in the morning, work during the day, dinner at night and quiet evenings together talking, reading, or watching television. Marriage is caring for children, watching over them in sickness, training them in the way they must go, sharing worry about them and pride in them."

Sometimes Bruce Lee was known to withdraw from the world, and it was at those times that Linda's importance to him became clear. "I remember one time we went to a beach party," recalled Bob Bremer. "Everyone was all out there drinking beer and everything. I look over in the middle of these people and there was Bruce and Linda sitting all by themselves. Bruce was kind of playing in the sand, and I thought, *'Damn! You would think that people would be over there talking to them.'* You know, they were all having a party and I thought maybe he didn't want to talk about anything. His mind was kind of stuck on that one gear (martial arts). You didn't know whether to feel sorry for him or to watch out." It was usually his wife who was able to bring Bruce Lee out of his shell and make him open up.

It has often been stated by those who knew Bruce Lee that his wife was his real source of strength. "I am fortunate – not because my film can break a record," said Bruce Lee, "but because I have a good wife, Linda. She is unsurpassed."

BRUCE LEE: HUMAN BEING

When I look around, I always learn something, and that is to always be yourself, express yourself, to have faith in yourself. Do not go out and look for a successful personality and duplicate him. They always copy mannerism; they never start from the root of their being: that is, how can I be me?

Bruce Lee

Bruce Lee is best remembered by those who knew him, not as a martial artist or movie star, but as a teacher and friend.

When Bruce Lee first arrived in Seattle, he began to develop a reputation for teaching gung fu. Soon Lee had many people wanting to study under him. One of those people was a 38-year-old Japanese American named Taky Kimura. Kimura spent five years in a United States internment camp during World War II and, after the war ended, suffered difficulty in getting a decent job under the shadow of post-war anti-Japanese sentiment. Demoralized, Kimura was seeking something to give him back his self-confidence. He found that in the young Bruce Lee, who became his mentor, spiritual guide, and best friend.

"All the time we were growing up, my mother and dad always said, 'Look, we're nothing but second-class citizens so don't ever put yourself in the mainstream of life because you are going to get

Bruce Lee was more than just a teacher to Taky Kimura. (Photo courtesy of Andy Kimura)

hurt,'" said Kimura. "We argued with them because the educational system told us that we were equal under the constitution. But then (when the war came along) all of a sudden, things changed and we were put in the internment camps, even though we were citizens. The Selective Service put us in the 4Y category, which was an alien classification, and they told us that there were rumors that they were going to take us and ship us off to some island as soon as they could get rid of us. Anyhow, they put us in camps.

"I came out and I was just a broken man because of this humiliation that occurred within myself. And then, in 1959, I had the wonderful honor of being in the right place at the right time to meet Bruce.

"He was 18, a typical teenager with all this boundless energy, telling dirty jokes and all that, and I was 36 and just mentally devastated. I couldn't relate to that, but he understood.

"Bruce came along and helped me out. He used to say, *'Jesus Christ, Kimura! Look at these clothes you're wearing! You look like an old man!'* And I would say, *'I'm clean, aren't I?'* But you know, he told me to wear different clothes and all this kind of stuff, and it was all a part of making me realize that I am a human being, no better or worse than anyone else. He told that repeatedly to me and (by teaching you the fundamentals of physicalness within yourself) obviously you start feeling better about yourself, when you know that you can do something. I think that that is one of the great things. Unfortunately, we all have to go through this process to understand what our capabilities are. But if you don't progress any further than that, then you're not going to get anywhere."

Bruce Lee had a wicked sense of humor as well. Because of his vision problems, Lee had to wear glasses or contacts. A student of his, who worked as an optometrist, made him colored contact lenses that he used to play jokes on unsuspecting people. In one instance, Bruce Lee put on white contact lenses and had his students lead him into a restaurant as if he was blind. In front of the waiter, he would let his hand hover across the menu and order in Chinese, which his students would then "translate" into a real order as if he was using some mystical Asian power to read the menu.

Sometimes when Bruce Lee went to the movies, he would wear a pair of bright red contact lenses. Lee would approach the ticket counter with his head turned down and order a ticket. As he paid for it, he would raise his head and the ticket counter would get the shock of their lives!

Bruce Lee was also quick to tell a joke. When asked why he did not smoke, Lee would reply he chewed gum instead, saying, "Many men smoke, but *Fu Manchu."*

Said Bruce Lee student Larry Hartsell: "He was a funny guy. He always had jokes. If he liked you, he'd do anything for you. He lived up on Roscomeare Road when I got out of Vietnam. I would go up and train at his home with Dan (Inosanto) and the rest of the guys. A lot of times, I would drive him to bookstores. He used to love all those old books on self-defense, some as old as the 1800s."

Bruce Lee student Jerry Poteet once spoke of a little trick Lee played on him during a visit to his teacher's home. He was in Bruce Lee's library, which had thousands of books. Lee was very particular about people messing with his books and had a sign on the shelf with the explicit order: *DO NOT TOUCH.* Poteet self-consciously kept his hands behind his back to avoid the temptation of picking up a book. "Suddenly, from the doorway Bruce called out my name and I turned to see a three-sectional staff flying through the air toward me. I reacted with a yell as it caught me full in the face, and then I realized it was made of foam rubber. Bruce roared at my reaction, and I said, *'Okay, you've had your fun now let me have mine.'* Bruce Lee knew I was dying to glance at the comments he made in the margins of his books, so he said, *'All right, but make sure you put every book back in its place.'* The joke was still on me, however, because as soon as I opened a book, I realized all his comments were written in Chinese."

Bruce Lee liked to "perform" for people he met. He enjoyed dazzling people by doing two-finger pushups. One of his favorite tricks was to ask a person to hold a dime in their up-turned palm. Lee then challenged the person to close their hand before he could get the dime. Inevitably, Bruce Lee would make his move and the person would quickly shut his hand, smug in the knowledge that he could still feel the dime in his palm. However, when the person opened his hand, he would find a penny where the dime had been! Lee demonstrated this trick to the producers of the *Kung Fu* television series, and they incorporated it into the show as the now famous "snatch the pebble from my hand" cliché.

At rest, Bruce Lee's incredible physique was not immediately apparent. One of his favorite sight gags was to stick his thumb in his mouth and act as if he was blowing himself up like a balloon. He would slowly flex his muscles, expand his lats, and tense his body. The resulting effect was that Bruce Lee appeared twice as big as he did the moment before.

Patrick Strong recalls Bruce Lee incorporating this into one of his practical jokes. "One time, I took Bruce to the Universal Health Studios in Seattle. The guy that managed the gym was a big muscle-head. I introduced him to Bruce, who was playing dumb. We were standing at this big rack of dumbbells. They went in size from three-pound dumbbells to 120-pound dumbbells. Bruce looked at them and said, *'Well, what are these for?'* So, this bodybuilder goes over and he picks up two ninety-pound dumbbells in each hand. He said, *'What we do with those, we do curls.'* He started showing Bruce how to do curls. *'This is how we do curls. As I curl this up, I'm building my bicep muscle. Do you see that?'* You saw this big muscle rippling on this guy. So, Bruce looked at him and he went over and picked up the three pounders, the ones for girls. Bruce did one rep and he groaned and sighed. He did a second rep and he got bigger. He did a third rep and his neck started to swell. He swelled up like a blowfish! The bodybuilder just stood there; he couldn't believe it! His eyes just bugged out! It was hysterical! Bruce just got bigger, and bigger, and bigger with each single rep, like you were pumping him full of air!

"Bruce turned to the guy, all pumped up, and said, *'Oh, this really works!'*"

As a teenager in Hong Kong, Bruce Lee had a number of encounters with British military men. Doug Palmer, a friend and student from Lee's Seattle years, remembers Lee telling him about one particular encounter. "The soldiers went around asking for it and Bruce didn't go out of his way to avoid it. He told me about one incident where he pretended to be very effeminate and uncoordinated. The person swung at him, and he blocked the punch in a very awkward way. In the end (as if the hit was an accident) he flicked the soldier in the groin. The soldier was rolling on the ground and Bruce walked away tittering. I asked Bruce why he did it that way. Bruce said, *'Well, if you beat up somebody, they know that you're stronger or better. They can accept it. But, if they think they've been beat up by a spastic, they'll never be able to live it down.'*"

Bruce Lee had little use for convention and felt that social etiquette should be natural and not forced. His wife, Linda, had to adjust to it, but she learned to admire him for it. For example, Linda said he thought that opening doors and bringing flowers were unimportant things. "These are merely actions; it is the thought that you have for a person which is important." She said that he never forgot birthdays and anniversaries and was very considerate.

One of Bruce Lee's eccentricities was the fact that he did not like to be casually touched by strangers. Bob Bremer recalls that element of Lee's personality. "If you came up like, *'Hi!'* (slapping him on the back), you made a mistake. You never touched him. If you're a friend of his, yeah, you could have touched him. But, if you didn't know him, that was a wrong thing to do. He was a wealthy Chinaman, and he didn't want any trash touching him. He told me, *'I like to fight. But in order to fight, I must let them touch my skin. If they touch my skin, I will hit their skin. If they hit my skin, I will crush their bones. If they crush my bones, I will take their life!'*"

Bruce Lee always took an active interest in the well-being of his students and friends. One of his students, Ted Wong, was shy and unassuming with little or no social life. Lee took him to a store, picked out nice clothes for him to wear, and then took him to a stylist to get a more attractive hairstyle. "Bruce always encouraged me to be myself and not be afraid," said Wong. "What he helped me with far exceeds what he taught me in martial art. He was a great person, and he gave me confidence."

Kareem Abdul-Jabbar shares Ted Wong's love for Bruce Lee. "I remember Bruce as a friend. The whole martial arts thing is secondary to our friendship."

Ted Wong said Bruce Lee helped bring Wong out of his shell and taught him to enjoy life.

"I guess the biggest thing I noticed about Bruce was that tremendous energy and unceasing drive to be the best," said Fred Sato. "He was always trying, adjusting, and learning; and I'm sure, till the day he passed away, he was trying to learn something."

Sato recalls the connection Bruce Lee had with children. "He would come over. I had two daughters (three and five at the time) who were completely entranced by Bruce. He would ask my three-year-old daughter, *'How old are you?'* She would run into the hall and then she would come back and say, *'I'm three.'* He would do that every time he came over. He would ask that same question until she finally stood there and told him how old she was. So, by the time she was four, she could figure it out. That taught me something about Bruce. He got the biggest kick out of that."

Sato said Bruce Lee was equally charming toward the elderly. "My mother-in-law was a first-generation Japanese. She spoke fluent Japanese and broken English." Sato said his mother-in-law was curious about Lee and would stand near the two during their conversations and listen.

"Bruce noticed that," said Sato, "so the next time he came over, all of a sudden he made a beeline for the kitchen and my mother-in-law was in there talking to him." They were discussing the written languages of Chinese and Japanese. "Somehow, they were communicating. He spent an hour with a much older person. Those things I remember about Bruce, the humanity of the man."

Sato notes that, for such a larger-than-life man, Bruce Lee could be pretty down to earth. "In the early sixties we couldn't afford to get soft drinks (you know, teacher's pay), so instead of soft drinks we had Kool-Aid. You know how far Kool-Aid goes. A package of Kool-

Aid would make half a gallon. It took me a long time to figure out it wasn't worth the amount of sugar you put into it. Anyway, Bruce drank a whole half-gallon of it! I don't know if he was being polite or what, but he said, *'I love Kool-Aid.'"*

Bruce Lee also gave self-defense tips to Sato's wife. "If there is a would-be rapist that comes at you, it's pretty simple: you wrap your arms and legs around him and start screaming. He'll be so startled – you're the attacker now!"

In January 1969, while the whole entertainment industry seemed to be conspiring against him, Bruce Lee sat down and put his goals on paper. That paper, titled "My Definite Chief Aim", would prove to be very prophetic. "I, Bruce Lee, will be the first highest paid oriental superstar in the United States. In return, I will give the most exciting performances and render the highest of quality in the capacity of an actor. Starting in 1970, I will achieve world fame and from then onward, till the end of 1980, I will have in my possession $10,000,000. I will live the way I please and achieve inner harmony and happiness."

Jhoon Rhee, the father of American Taekwondo, recalls being with Bruce Lee when he wrote his historic one-page promise to himself. "At the time, I really didn't question whether he would manage to achieve his aim or not. I just knew that, with his quality, talent, determination, and commitment in the martial arts, things would happen."

"Bruce had a lot of affirmations, a lot of which came true," Larry Hartsell remembered. "He had them written down. I've seen a few of them. He wanted to be one of the biggest movie stars around. That came about when he outgrossed Steve McQueen's *Bullet* with *Enter the Dragon*. Bruce was very ambitious, which was good."

While he had many virtues, Bruce Lee was not without fault. One noticeable fault was his temper. He was the first to admit that he had a short fuse. Once, on a return visit to Hong Kong after *The Green Hornet* was canceled, Lee was nearly hit while walking across a street. The man in the car started verbally abusing Bruce Lee with no idea to whom he was talking. "I wanted to drag him out of the car and break him into pieces, but I knew I couldn't do that," said Bruce Lee. "Instead, I reached down and grabbed his nose and tried to twist it off. I felt a lot better."

Bob Bremer recalls one time when he narrowly avoided Bruce Lee's wrath. "When I am talking about fighting somebody, I'd say *BLAM!* or *SMACK!* Bruce had a different set of distinctive sounds.

Bruce Lee's student Bob Bremer fondly remembers Lee as a true friend and a decent human being.

He had a Chinese one, he'd say *'FONG...'*.

"I thought that was kind of funny. I had never heard of *FONG* before. There was a blackboard in the Chinatown school building, and I would write *'FONG?'* and I'd put a big question mark.

"The next time I turned around somebody had erased it. Who the hell erased that? I'd write it again. *'FONG?.* Big question mark. I turned around and it was gone again! *'Man!'* I said. I did it the third time and went back to practicing. Well, we're working out and I hear somebody saying *'Goddamn, son of a bitch!'* Bruce was over there furiously erasing the blackboard. *'Somebody keeps writing FONG on this damn board!'* I had no idea that that would make him mad."

After Bruce Lee established himself as a star in Hong Kong, he was forced to deal with the constant problems that come with fame. Once Lee found a man in his back yard in the Kowloon Tong province of Hong Kong. The man breached the security of Bruce Lee's home by scaling a fence in the back. He told Lee he wanted to see how good Bruce Lee really was. Lee was livid that someone would have the audacity to invade his home and potentially jeopardize the safety of his family. Lee said hello to the intruder with what he described as "the hardest sidekick I had ever given anybody."

Bruce Lee was often challenged once he became famous, but

generally, he ignored his challengers. In a 1971 interview with journalist Ted Thomas, Lee was asked about the various challenges that were made. "When I first learned martial art, I too challenged many established instructors. And, of course, some others have challenged me also," said Bruce Lee. "But what I have learned is that challenging means one thing and that is: *What is your reaction? How does it get to you?* If you are secure within yourself, you treat it very lightly, because you ask yourself: *Am I afraid of that man? Do I have any doubts that he might get me?*"

Bruce Lee was also concerned about the possibility that his martial art movies would influence the younger generation to violence. Lee knew that if it was done responsibly then there would be no problem. "I never want to make a movie for the sake of cruelty," he said. "I will first examine the reasons why the characters have to fight. Are these reasons sufficient? If not, I will not join in. Because martial arts is my career, I want to use it as a means to express my ideals. A real fighter should fight for righteousness." In the movie *Fist of Fury,* for example, Lee insisted that his character die at the end of the movie, since there must be a balance for the character's mission of vengeance. "A man who has killed many people must take responsibility for it. What I am trying to prove is that a man living by violence dies by violence."

Though Bruce Lee loved his teacher Yip Man, they had a falling out in the last few years of Yip Man's life. Sifu Yip Man shared his country's distrust of foreigners and was very much against teaching gung fu to them. So, when he found out Bruce Lee was teaching the *gwei-lo* his art, he was extremely unhappy. Lee, for his part, was unapologetic. He believed that all people were basically the same and that, through gung fu, he could introduce the West to the Chinese culture and bring about greater understanding between people. The two never resolved their differences, and Bruce Lee did not even attend Yip Man's funeral.

When interviewed by Canadian journalist Pierre Berton in Hong Kong on December 9, 1971, Bruce Lee was asked whether he considered himself an American or Chinese, to which Lee answered: "You know how I like to think of myself? As a human being. Because, and I don't want to sound like *'as Confucius says,'* but under the sky, under the heavens, there is but one family. It just so happens that people are different."

Through it all, Bruce Lee was still teacher and guide to his friends. At the time he was filming *Enter the Dragon*, Bruce Lee's friend Taky Kimura called him from the United States with a personal crisis: Kimura's marriage was falling apart, and he was despondent and suicidal. "I lost two brothers a month apart and then my wife left me," said Kimura.

Bruce Lee told his friend, "Taky, I haven't met your wife, but I've counseled you before. You must do everything in your power to solve the thing but, at some point in time, you may just have to walk on." Lee was telling Taky Kimura that if nature dictated that the marriage was over, going against it would only bring further unhappiness. Lee was expressing the Taoist philosophy of *wu-wei* or following the course of nature without resisting it. "Walk on," he would tell Kimura, "Walk on."

"Life is an ever-flowing process and somewhere on the path some unpleasant things will pop up – it might leave a scar – but then life is flowing on, and like running water, when it stops, it grows stale. Go bravely on, my friend, because each experience teaches us a lesson."

On July 20, 1973, Bruce Lee died of a cerebral edema, three weeks before the opening of *Enter the Dragon*, three weeks before he would gain worldwide fame.

Bruce Lee was buried at Lakeview Cemetery in Seattle, Washington. The casket was covered in white, red, and yellow flowers making up the Jeet Kune Do symbol. The pallbearers were Steve McQueen, James Coburn, Bruce Lee's brother Robert, and Lee's top student, Dan Inosanto. At the gravesite, James Coburn had the last words: *"Farewell, brother. It has been an honor to share this space with you. As a friend and a teacher, you have given to me, have brought my physical, spiritual, and psychological selves together. Thank you. May peace be with you."*

Bruce Lee's wife, Linda, summed up Lee's character when she said, "There would have been no greater compliment that you could say to Bruce than to say, *'You are a real human being.'* That's what he wanted to be."

BRUCE LEE: LEGEND

Through the ages, the end of heroes is always the same as ordinary men. They all died and gradually faded away in the memory of man. But when we are still alive, we have to understand ourselves, discover ourselves, and express ourselves.

Bruce Lee

The legend of Bruce Lee began the minute he died. Like James Dean or John F. Kennedy, the abrupt passing of so bright a star tends to cause the memory of the person to take on a life of its own. Lee's case was no different.

The Hong Kong press both helped and hindered this evolution. In the beginning, the press praised Bruce Lee as a shining example of humanity, but, toward the end, something changed. The newspapers in Hong Kong began criticizing Lee in the last few months of his life. The press grew tired of what they perceived as Bruce Lee's cockiness, and a few high-profile missteps on Lee's part (his failure to attend Yip Man's funeral, his behavior in a televised interview, and reportedly pulling a knife on director Lo Wei), fueled the gossip mill. The Hong Kong press of the time did not have the same journalistic ethics of its American counterpoint, and while Woodward and Bernstein were uncovering Watergate, the Hong Kong press

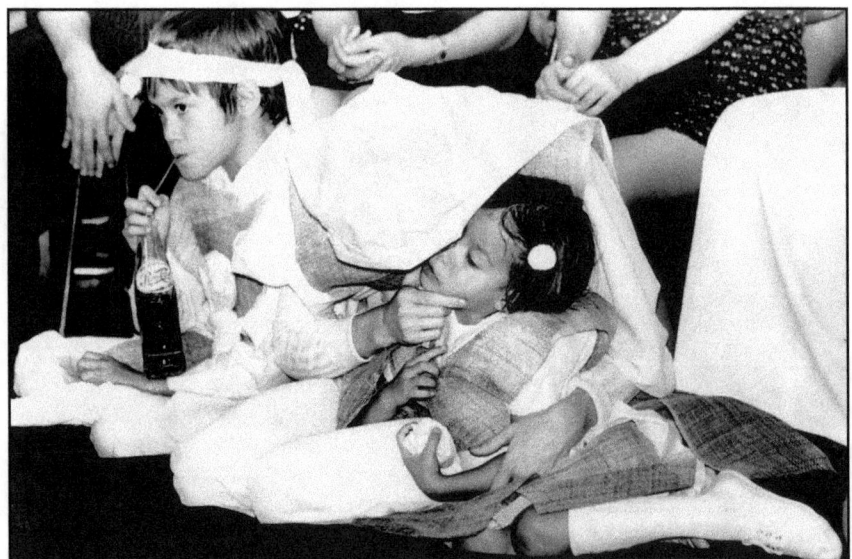

Bruce Lee's widow Linda Lee comforts daughter, Shannon, while son, Brandon, looks at the crowd gathered for Bruce Lee's Hong Kong memorial service on July 25, 1973. The three wear traditional Chinese mourning gowns. (South China Morning Post)

was spreading salacious tabloid gossip about the biggest Chinese star. In one absurd example, a Hong Kong newspaper boldly proclaimed, "BRUCE LEE CONNECTED TO MASS MURDER". The ridiculous basis of the story was that Bruce Lee's student, Kareem Abdul-Jabbar, bought a house in California that was the scene of a triple homicide years before he purchased it. That was Lee's only connection to the event, but that did not stop the press in Hong Kong from exerting a little "artistic license" in their coverage of Bruce Lee. Where they were once overflowing with praise after the release of the *Big Boss* and *Fist of Fury,* they now found maligning Lee their new favorite pastime.

In life, Bruce Lee learned to take the barbs on his character in stride, though secretly the comments made in the press were personally hurtful to him. Now that Bruce Lee was dead, the press had *carte blanche* with his memory. The press had a field day when they discovered that Bruce Lee died in the apartment of actress Betty Ting Pei. Raymond Chow and Linda Lee's attempts to cover it up – by concocting a story that Bruce Lee died at home – only added fuel to the fire. The story backfired after a clever reporter checked the ambulance records and traced Lee's ambulance back to Betty Ting Pei's apartment. Raymond Chow and Linda Lee's falsified story appeared to be a cover-up, and the press showered the Hong Kong public with reports of Bruce Lee's "affair" with Betty Ting Pei and his mysterious death in her "fragrant chamber".

In truth, the citizens of Hong Kong never really accepted Bruce Lee's *gwei-lo* wife, and they were more than willing to embrace the idea that Bruce Lee died in the bed of a woman who was authentically Chinese. While Lee's family would have preferred he married a Chinese, the Chinese public openly resented that he had not. The Hong Kong press was constantly trying to connect Bruce Lee with various Chinese women, and saying that Betty Ting Pei was his paramour would be a victory against the West. Betty Ting Pei, for her part, only added fuel to the fire. Enjoying her newfound celebrity, she went on record proclaiming her "affair" with Bruce Lee, milking it for all it was worth. The highlight of her efforts was a starring role in a soft porn movie titled *Bruce Lee: His Last Days, His Last Nights* that detailed her supposed relationship with Lee, a role that did not require a lot of acting (or clothing for that matter). A few years later, she found religion and recanted her story, saying that she was wrong to say such things and that she and Bruce Lee were only close friends.

The coroner's report stating that traces of Cannabis were found in Bruce Lee's body also fueled rumors about his drug use. Though Lee was not publicly known to smoke or even drink alcohol, in truth Cannabis was only one of many recreational drugs that Bruce Lee was doing. Through a variety of suppliers – including his student and *Fist of Fury* co-star Bob Baker and his Hollywood student James Coburn – Lee was smuggling into Hong Kong and consuming considerable amounts of Cocaine, highly potent Nepalese Hash Oil, and psychedelic drugs like LSD and Psilocybin. None of this drug use, beyond the Cannabis found in Bruce Lee's stomach contents, was known to the coroner or the individuals conducting the inquest into Bruce Lee's death. Only those closest to him, including his wife, knew of Bruce Lee's recreational drug use. Said Van Williams, his co-star in *The Green Hornet:* "When he was here, he did not smoke cigarettes. He couldn't stand to be around people who did. He never took a drink that I ever saw. He didn't smoke pot."

Linda Lee, for her part, was trying her best to quell the conjecture that was running rampant about Bruce Lee. It was bad enough that she had just lost her husband, but now she was having to defend his memory and protect her children at the same time. Linda made a heartfelt plea to the Hong Kong press to let his memory rest. "All that matters is that he is gone," she said, but the press refused to listen.

In August 1973, *Enter the Dragon* was released in the United States and became an instant hit. Bruce Lee was now a dominating force in the world of Hollywood, only he was not there to enjoy it or control it.

Mark Cole of Mobile Alabama remembers the Bruce Lee craze that followed the release of *Enter the Dragon*. "I was in high school, and it was just phenomenal to see this man doing the things he was doing with his body, with his martial arts. I was extremely inspired, and I went and watched all of his movies. I bought books about him and studied him. It was hard to believe that he had died."

Golden Harvest producer Raymond Chow was quick to catch on to the new Bruce Lee fever, as was Run Run Shaw. Shaw bankrolled Betty Ting Pei's movie about Lee, a gesture that surely brought Run Run Shaw a great deal of personal satisfaction, as Lee refused to work for him in life and in death was making him money.

For Linda Lee, it became imperative that her husband be remembered for his good qualities; it was equally important that she preserve her control over all things Bruce Lee. After all, she had two children to support and raise, and they should rightly be the benefactors of Lee's fame and his ability to generate money.

To generate income for her family and control the narrative about her husband, Linda Lee quickly published her own Bruce Lee biography. The book, *Bruce Lee: The Man Only I Knew,* was released less than two years after his death. It established many of the commonly-held beliefs about Bruce Lee, some of them untrue, that endure to this day.

There were also legal issues to address. Bruce Lee's attorney, Adrian Marshall, was instrumental in helping Linda Lee maintain control over the Bruce Lee Estate. Everyone seemed to be trying to profit off of Bruce Lee, and it was Marshall who made sure that Linda Lee and her children received what was due to them. In proxy, Marshall became the protector of the Lee family that Bruce Lee could no longer be.

Despite Marshall's considerable legal wrangling, there were some things he could not stop. Being a public figure, it was nearly impossible to stop people from exploiting some variation of Bruce Lee's likeness for their own purposes. A slew of imitators emerged, turning Lee's memory into a joke – just as Elvis Presley impersonators have done to the memory of the King of Rock and Roll.

Linda Lee, widow of Bruce Lee, on a book tour in London in February 1975 to promote her book, Bruce Lee: The Man Only I Knew. (Alamy)

In 1975, Linda Lee authorized the publication of the *Tao of Jeet Kune Do,* a book compiled from Bruce Lee's notes. It became an immediate international bestseller. The book was described as a compendium of Lee's philosophical opinions on the nature of life and martial arts, as well as an overview of his combat methods and training regimen.

While advertised as the original thoughts and writings of Bruce Lee, virtually the entirety of the *Tao of Jeet Kune Do* is composed of unattributed quotations from other authors. This does not appear, initially, to have been the result of a conscious effort of the publisher or the Lee Estate to defraud consumers. The editor hired to compile the book, Gilbert Johnson, functioned from the understanding that the notes given to him for the purpose of compiling the book originated with Bruce Lee. And while Lee wrote copious notes for his own use derived from books in his expansive personal library, he did not bother to document the sources for the majority of those notes.

Nonetheless, the sale of the *Tao of Jeet Kune Do* was halted almost immediately upon its publication, after a reader named Joseph Snyder identified that parts of the book were taken from other sources. Acknowledgments were added to the front of the book for those authors identified by Snyder and the book resumed publication, but requests to acknowledge further discoveries over the years (by both Snyder and others) were rebuffed by the publisher and the Bruce Lee Estate.

When a public figure reaches the status of legend, it is inevitable that they will receive the biographical film treatment, and Bruce Lee was no different. A few Bruce Lee biographical films were made in Hong Kong during the years that immediately followed Lee's death. Interestingly, they all tended omit the fact that Bruce Lee had a Caucasian wife, some choosing to ignore his marriage altogether.

Then, in 1993, Universal Pictures released the first movie biography on Bruce Lee authorized by the Bruce Lee Estate. *Dragon: The Bruce Lee Story* was adapted from Linda Lee's book *Bruce Lee: The Man Only I Knew*. Linda Lee, now remarried and named Linda Lee Cadwell, worked closely with producer Rafaella DeLaurentis and director Rob Cohen to ensure that the motion picture would capture the spirit of the real Bruce Lee.

"Bruce was a driven man – I mean incredibly driven," said Rob Cohen. "I think he was unique because he stood in the middle of two fantastically powerful cultures (the Chinese culture and the American culture), so that he was able to single-handedly pull the two cultures together, to make both sides understand each other better."

Cast as Bruce Lee was Hawaiian native Jason Scott Lee. The decision was controversial given that the actor was not a martial artist. Cohen held firm on the casting. "I felt that if you take a martial artist and teach him to act it won't work, but you could teach an actor the martial arts and, with a little luck, you might get someone who can pull it off. What we got was a lot of luck!"

Jason Scott Lee portrayed a Bruce Lee of great passion, insight, and intelligence. His inspiring portrayal made the movie a success and allowed the real Bruce Lee to shine through.

For the actor, portraying Bruce Lee profoundly changed him. "I learned I was capable, that there was the possibility of achieving in a short amount of time a breakthrough of the personal barriers – physically, mentally, and spiritually," he said.

After wrapping production on the film, Jason Scott Lee continued to study Jeet Kune Do under (Bruce Lee student and the fight choreographer for the movie) Jerry Poteet, and even became an instructor in Bruce Lee's art. "The biggest and most grateful treasure I've had and still cherish is in the art of what Bruce taught and what Jerry has been passing out to me."

THE LEGACY OF BRUCE LEE

I have come to discover through earnest personal experience and dedicated learning that ultimately the greatest help is self-help; that there is no other help but self-help---doing one's best, dedicating one's self wholeheartedly to a given task, which happens to have no end but is an ongoing process. I have done a lot during these years of my process. As well in my process, I have changed from self-image actualization to self-actualization, from blindly following propaganda, organized truths, etc., to searching internally for the cause of my ignorance.

Bruce Lee

Of greatest importance to the legend of Bruce Lee is his legacy as a teacher, a motivator, and an inspiration. It is here that his impact on the world is best represented. Through the students of his martial art, his fans, and his family, Lee's contributions continue to grow. For many of these people, Bruce Lee was not simply a star or a teacher; he was a role model whose example and encouragement inspired them on to greater success.

Chief among the people who are responsible for perpetuating the legacy of Bruce Lee are the students of his art. One of the most important of these has been Dan Inosanto of Los Angeles. Inosanto was one of only three instructors Bruce Lee designated during his lifetime and was the principal instructor at Lee's Los Angeles school. Inosanto worked closely with Bruce Lee during the period in

Bruce Lee facing his student Dan Inosanto in a scene from Game of Death. *Inosanto was the instructor of Bruce Lee's Los Angeles school.* (South China Morning Post)

which he developed Jeet Kune Do.

When Bruce Lee died, Inosanto stood to gain both fame and fortune as the "next Bruce Lee". Inosanto was approached by businessmen about franchising Jeet Kune Do as a chain of schools. He refused to do so on the grounds that it would not be what Bruce Lee wanted, even though it would have made him financially successful. Movie producers also turned to Dan Inosanto to fill the gap left by Bruce Lee in the motion picture industry, as his experience and connection to Lee would be enough alone to sell a movie. Inosanto turned them down as well, because he did not want to cheapen what his teacher gave him by riding on his coattails.

In keeping with his commitment to Bruce Lee, Inosanto continued to research and explore the martial arts, evolving (as a martial artist) along his own path as he believed Lee would have wanted. At his Inosanto Academy in Los Angeles, Inosanto continues to teach the fighting methods of Bruce Lee under the name of Jun Fan Gung Fu, while at the same time teaching Jeet Kune Do as a philosophical approach to fighting, a "concept" that the student can use to fully maximize his fighting potential.

First Generation Students

Like Inosanto, *Larry Hartsell* was a student of Kenpo master Ed Parker when he met Bruce Lee. As in Inosanto's case, Bruce Lee awakened Hartsell to his true potential.

Larry Hartsell and Bruce Lee met in 1964. Hartsell was practicing in Ed Parker's school when Bruce Lee and his wife entered the school. Lee was friends with Parker and often dropped by. Taking note of Hartsell, Bruce Lee approached him and asked him if he would like to spar.

Said Larry Hartsell: "My initial reaction was that he was a little cocky. Then I sparred with him, and I couldn't touch him. I said to myself, *Something's wrong here!* So, I asked Bruce if I could be his student. He said yes. So basically, that is how I met Bruce. You couldn't mess with Bruce."

For Larry Hartsell, it was very inspiring to train with Bruce Lee. "He had a lot of charisma, a lot of energy. He'd make you want to put out your best. I compare him to Vince Lombardi, a good football coach. He made you want to give it all you've got."

Hartsell said that Bruce Lee's teaching and training was very practical and very intense. "One of the common misconceptions people have about Bruce is that what he did in the movies is what he taught in class. The movies were choreographed, and his training was more geared toward actuality, like in combat: reaction time, reflexes, etc. There wasn't a lot of jumping up eight feet over walls and stuff. That was for the Hong Kong movie set. One was for combat; one was for the screen."

Larry Hartsell recalled the day he heard Bruce Lee was dead. "It was a very sad day. I didn't believe it at first. Dan (Inosanto) phoned me in North Carolina (where I was living at the time) and told me it was true."

Hartsell was too upset to attend the funeral. "I was invited, but I didn't go. I just went up into the mountains and spent some time by myself."

Larry Hartsell eventually moved back to California, where he continued his training with Dan Inosanto. "He's just like Bruce, always training," said Hartsell about Inosanto. "Guro Dan is an instructor in about 15 systems of Kali and Escrima, and that's what makes it fun. There's no ending to martial arts. Once you think you have it all, you have nothing. So, we keep going, even at our age. Basically, that's the way Bruce Lee was."

Larry Hartsell demonstrating grappling techniques at one of his many seminars. (Photo courtesy of Leif T. Røbekk)

Hartsell tried to inspire his students the way that Bruce Lee inspired him. "The way Bruce motivated and inspired me was in his teaching: how quick he was, his conditioning, the way he reacted, and the way he trained inspired me quite a bit. I try to pass that on to my students through showing different techniques and raising the energy level. In other words, making people want to go for it! I train fighters differently than I do people at seminars. Currently, I have two fighters that I want fighting in Japan. I also work with fighters like Randy Couture, who has won the Ultimate Fighting Championship twice. So that's why I have to keep on top of it."

When asked about the reason some people have had negative things to say about Bruce Lee since his death, Hartsell replied: "It could be anything. It could be their own ego, their own insecurities about themselves, knowing what Bruce was. Anyone can talk about the dead, build themselves up to be this and that. I never do. I firmly admit it, just like when I did my recent workshop. I had a Sambo stylist – a big Russian guy – as a guest. A lot of these 'black belts' would watch, but they wouldn't jump in there. I was the first one to jump in. Let's get the knowledge! You've got to be non-ego. In other words, Bruce was right: your cup has to be empty before I can fill it. *Anybody.* You know, I jump in there and work out in those classes. I don't say, *'I'm Larry Hartsell and I don't need to know anymore.'* Life is a continuing process. You should learn all you can."

Hartsell's own evolution as a martial artist took him down a path that focused a great deal of attention on the grappling aspects of fighting. "When I was involved in law enforcement, I studied the locking control techniques over the years. When I was a bouncer and a sheriff's deputy, I was in fights that ended up on the ground. As you get older, you might lose your kicks and your punches and your reaction time, but *grappling* you keep."

Despite his own involvement with Bruce Lee and Lee's martial art, Larry Hartsell remained surprised by how popular Lee has become, though he understood why. "He was the forerunner of everything that is going on today. He broke with tradition and found his own path to the top of the mountain."

Larry Hartsell passed away on August 20, 2007, from liver cancer. He was 65 years old.

Another original Bruce Lee student is *Patrick Strong*. Strong met Lee in Seattle in early 1961. His friend, Doug Palmer, was training under Lee and often told Strong about the young Chinese gung fu prodigy. Strong decided to go see what Bruce Lee was all about.

"I went to watch a workout," said Patrick Strong. "I was boxing at the Cherry Street Gym at the time, which had some professional fighters, such as Archie Moore. I wanted to see what was going on. I thought I had seen some really fast guys, but when I saw Bruce, I had never seen anything that fast before – hands that could move like that. *Blinding speed.* So, I immediately signed up.

"I've trained in martial arts ever since then and with a lot of different people, but what struck me most about Bruce (other than his blinding speed and his effectiveness) was that he could express himself with martial arts as in philosophy. His philosophy was an extension of his art.

"For example, he would teach the *Tan Sao,* which is the palm-up hand in Wing Chun, and in that hand is another principle called the immovable elbow principle. He would describe that elbow, that it would fit one fist's length away from the body, and if that elbow were ever pushed in any further than that then your structure would be destroyed. It was the holding place and under no circumstances would you let that be compromised. Then he would turn around and apply that to things in life: there is a point (in life) that you will not go beyond, such as a business negotiation. There is a point where you're going to hold firm, you're not going to go beyond that point, and so you hold there. Once you go beyond that point, you lose;

you lose what you set out to accomplish. So, he would do that all of the time. He would describe his art in philosophical and in meaningful terms.

"Then in that same hand, the palm-up hand, he would describe the arm as neither bent nor straight. To bend it would have been an extreme as in too much Yin; to keep it straight would be too much Yang. So, it was neither bent nor straight. When I was 18 years old, and he would be talking like that, I didn't know what he was talking about! Here's some guy describing an arm that is neither bent nor straight, saying it's both bent and straight.

"It was the first time I ever heard anybody talk like that," recalled Patrick Strong. "When I went off to college, the first courses I signed up for were philosophy. Then the stuff started making a lot of sense."

"I spent a great deal of time listening to Bruce. I listened and hung on every single word he said, and some of those terms have gotten lost over the years. A few years ago, I was up in Seattle visiting with Taky (Kimura). I started talking about non-intention, and Taky didn't know what I was talking about. I said, *'Don't you remember how Bruce described how you arrive at non-intention by being like a set of keys that lie on the top of a table? The table moves, the keys fall...'* And he said *'Oh, I forgot about that!'* So, what has happened, over the years, is that everything has gone toward non-telegraphing (where you do not give an indication you are about to strike). But the key to Bruce's speed was non-intention. In non-intention, you strike without the intention to strike. You eliminate the intention. So, when they filmed *Enter the Dragon*, the editor re-ran the fight footage of Bruce over and over – particularly the scene with Bruce and Bob Wall where they would touch in cross-hands position. Bruce would move in with a *Pak Sao* and hit Bob Wall. The editor noticed that no matter how much he slowed that film down, there was absolutely no preparation from Bruce at all, absolutely no telegraphing. Well, the way Bruce was able to achieve this was through non-intention. The editor said, *'There wasn't like you could see a place where he began to make his movement. He was here one second and the next second he was there.'* There wasn't anything that wound up to that move at all. It just happened."

The highest point of non-intention is where the actions and responses become autonomic and instantaneous. Patrick Strong once asked Bruce Lee how he would plead to a judge if he were ever forced to kill someone. According to Strong, Lee said he would, of course, plead *not guilty* because he didn't kill the man.

"I would say I didn't do it," Bruce Lee told Pat Strong, "*It did it.*"

Patrick Strong said Bruce Lee expressed this concept in his movies. "When he did *The Big Boss,* there was a scene where he is fighting a fellow in an ice factory. He hits the man in the abdomen and then he grabs his fist and looks at it like it was a thing that was unleashed, that it did it by itself. He didn't hit this guy, the weapon used itself. That's the idea exactly. For example, when you're driving down the street and a child runs out in front of you, your foot just goes to the brake. You don't intend to put your foot on the brake, you don't prepare to put it on the brake, it just goes to the brake, it just happens. No intention.

Patrick Strong, who studied under Bruce Lee during his Seattle years.

"Bruce's best analogy for that was the keys on the edge of the table. When the table moves, the keys fall. They don't think about falling; they don't prepare to fall. They just *fall.* Now in martial arts that's very meaningful."

Patrick Strong believes that the time for Bruce Lee's martial art may have arrived. "I think now is a good time for people to take a look at Lee's art. Today, martial arts are evolving, and you have a lot of cross training fighters because it is no holds barred. People are becoming real conscious of what works and what doesn't work, and there are some very good things that can be gleaned from Bruce's research."

Second Generation Students

One of the most popular and respected second-generation Jeet Kune Do practitioners is Burton Richardson. In addition to being a certified instructor in Jun Fan Gung Fu and Jeet Kune Do Concepts under Dan Inosanto, Richardson is also certified in the martial art of Filipino Kali (under Inosanto), Thai Boxing (under Master Chai

Second-generation student Burton Richardson says that Bruce Lee has inspired him to pursue his own personal evolution in the martial arts and in life. (Photo courtesy of Burton Richardson)

Sirisute), and the Indonesian art of Pentjak Silat (under Pendekar Paul de Thouars). Richardson also spent time in Manila, where he earned instructor rank in Kali Illustrisimo under Grandmaster Antonio Illustrisimo and Master Tony Diego.

Burton Richardson grew up in Carson, California. "I was lucky in that the house I grew up in was less than a mile from the original Kali/Jun Fan Gung Fu Academy run by Dan Inosanto and Richard Bustillo. I was interested in martial arts since I saw "Kato" as a young boy in *The Green Hornet* TV series, but it was years later that I learned that Bruce Lee played Kato. Despite my interest, I was not allowed to take martial arts until I graduated from high school in 1980. At that time, I was finally able to go to the Academy and begin my training. I have been training ever since in a variety of martial arts, using Bruce Lee's philosophy as a guide.

"A friend of mine in high school is the one who actually got me hooked on Bruce Lee's art. She shared books with me and told me about the Academy where she trained. When I went to see a class, I was surprised at what I saw. The students were wearing sweatpants, t-shirts, and athletic shoes; music was playing, and everyone was training very hard. They went from kicking the shield, to punching focus mitts, to weaponry. It was a very relaxed athletic environment that reminded me more of sports training than the militaristic traditional methods that I had seen. I was hooked!"

Richardson feels that truthfulness and a lack of ego are essential to becoming a successful Jeet Kune Do practitioner. "Honesty is the most important aspect of Jeet Kune Do. I must be honest with myself. I must admit that I don't know everything, and that what I am teaching today is not the end-all, be-all of the martial arts. This way,

I admit that there is always room for improvement, and I will go on researching a better way. If I fool myself into thinking that I know everything, then there is no need for growth, stagnation occurs, and I will become more interested in martial arts politics than martial arts practice. I must be honest in my teaching, because without it, I will have no integrity. I must let my students know that the only way to really be good is to practice correctly and consistently over a long period of time. They must spar hard in all of the ranges to understand the pressure of a real fight. Without this tough training, they will never really understand the art. It would be dishonest for me to tell my students that, to be good, they just have to memorize a set number of techniques and be able to demonstrate them on a cooperative training partner. I would have more students, but I know that is wrong. If a student ever gets into a tough altercation, he or she will discover the ineffectiveness of this training method in a most painful manner. Honesty often means taking the most difficult path, but the road is not crowded, and the views are incredible."

Burton Richardson was inspired and influenced a great deal by his instructor, Dan Inosanto. "Dan Inosanto is one of the most generous people I have ever met. He is always thinking of others, putting their wellbeing ahead of his own. He sacrifices so greatly to learn various arts, then gives it to his students freely. He is a great teacher in that he can teach a technique, that would normally take days to learn, and break it down in an understandable way. He is constantly researching different arts or training with various instructors in the same art to get different perspectives. He feels a duty to share what he has learned, because he wants to honor his teachers and better his students. Add to this, the fact that he is very humble and an extraordinarily nice person, and you have the one and only Dan Inosanto. What more could you ask for in a teacher?

"Dan Inosanto could have stopped training years ago and retained his status as one of the greatest martial artists of our time. He had enough material to teach for the next 300 years, but no! He is on a quest to be the best that he can be. At the age of 58, he put on a white belt and took up Brazilian Ju Jitsu. Why? Because he recognized that there were things that he didn't understand, and that the training could make he and his students better. Moreover, he has encouraged me to study with everyone I can. He put my learning and progress ahead of just trying to keep me as a student. That is loyalty from the top down, and this is why he deserves loyalty from myself and from all of his other students. He is an exemplary instructor."

Richardson found that the influence of Bruce Lee on his life grew beyond the martial arts. "Bruce Lee's simple concept of exploring different methods and then using what works for the individual is the cornerstone of my martial arts and everyday philosophy. I am always looking for ways to improve my home life, and I am not afraid to try new things. For example, my wife Sarah and I moved to Hawaii from Los Angeles. She is originally from a tropical island in the Indian Ocean, and I love Hawaii, so we made the decision and moved in less than three months! We didn't indulge in self-doubt or look for reasons to stay in Los Angeles. Instead, we looked at all of the positive benefits that we would gain and concentrated on those. This is how Bruce Lee approached his training. It may be easier to stick with the style of martial arts that you are comfortable with, but there may be better methods out there. You have to go out and try the different arts, even if it is very difficult at first. In the end, you will be richer for the experience, just as Sarah and I are very glad that we relocated. It wasn't easy, but we are reaping the rewards every day."

Another second-generation student of Bruce Lee's art of Jeet Kune Do is *Lamar Davis II*. The Jeet Kune Do instructor from Birmingham Alabama has been training in martial arts since he was 10. "I first saw Bruce Lee as Kato in *The Green Hornet* TV series. It was seeing Kato that inspired me to want to learn martial arts. I faithfully watched every episode of *The Green Hornet* series just to see what awesome moves that Kato was going to perform next. I didn't know exactly what it was that he was doing, but I knew that it looked good, and I wanted to learn it. Then I saw some early articles in *Black Belt Magazine*, which I still have today, talking about Kato and his unique method of fighting, *Jeet Kune Do*. Needless to say, I was extremely excited to get my hands on this information! When the episode of *Longstreet* called "The Way of the Intercepting Fist" aired, I was sitting in front of the TV set, mesmerized by the fact that Bruce Lee was right there in front of me, basically playing himself and explaining many of the principles of his incredible art of Jeet Kune Do. This just completely blew me away.

"From that moment on, I set out to learn everything I could about the man and his art. Even today, when something new on Bruce Lee is released, I still feel the same excitement that I felt as a teenager sitting in front of the television that night. I can't wait to get my hands on it and see if there is something new for me to learn!

Second-generation student Lamar M. Davis II says that being a part of preserving Bruce Lee's martial arts legacy and sutdying under Bruce Lee's original students has been a very rewarding experience. (Photo courtesy of Lamar Davis)

"Bruce Lee inspired me to keep on training hard and work to be the best that I can possibly be. No matter how good he got, he always felt that he could be better. No matter how fast he got, he always felt that he could be faster. That's dedication! I am always telling my students that, if Bruce Lee always felt he could be better, what gives us any right to say that we're as good as we can get? If watching him move doesn't inspire someone to work harder, nothing will."

For Lamar Davis, the most gratifying part of his experience with Jeet Kune Do is being part of the process that keeps Bruce Lee's art and memory alive. "I am most appreciative for being allowed to be a part of the martial arts lineage that I come from. Having trained with 15 of Bruce Lee's original students, I have truly been blessed to learn as much as I have about the man and his art. Although I never got to meet him, the next best thing is to be a second-generation student. For this privilege, I will thank God every day for the rest of my life. The single most important thing to me now, though, is the fact that I can teach this art to others and help preserve the legacy of Bruce Lee. I am definitely trying to do my part to spread the original teachings of Bruce Lee and keep his memory alive."

Original Jeet Kune Do Vs. Jeet Kune Do Concepts

Several years after the death of Bruce Lee, a schism developed among the teachers and practitioners of Lee's martial art of Jeet Kune Do. Some of Lee's original students took exception to Dan Inosanto and his students incorporating techniques into the art that were not practiced by Bruce Lee during his lifetime. Those who were critical of this practice feared that the additions would dilute the effectiveness of Lee's martial art, would not represent the choices Lee himself would have made had he not died, and would complicate the historical preservation of Jeet Kune Do. Inosanto, for his part, argued that Jeet Kune Do is not a "style" of fighting but rather a philosophical approach to fighting; an avenue of self-exploration that is not limited to a certain group of techniques but only to that which proves effective. Bruce Lee's art soon found itself divided into two groups: advocates of *Original Jeet Kune Do* and advocates of *Jeet Kune Do Concepts*.

Richard Torres, a Jeet Kune Do instructor from upstate New York and one of the most prominent advocates for Original Jeet Kune Do, explained the basic idea behind his preferred approach. "Jeet Kune Do is a total martial arts system, expressed by the human body scientifically, to try to achieve the maximum amount of effectiveness with the minimum amount of energy. The idea of learning in this art is constant drilling to hack away the bad habits (the unessentials) and sharpen the tools. It is not a matter of adding more and more styles but hacking away the unessentials. Jeet Kune Do is based on learning the martial tools correctly without delving into any style or discipline."

Unlike the Original Jeet Kune Do approach, the Jeet Kune Do Concepts approach embraces the exploration of other styles of fighting. "Jeet Kune Do Concepts is the ability to adapt and adjust to what is useful and what is not useful," said Larry Hartsell. "You owe allegiance of knowledge to yourself, meaning that there's no two people who are built the same, no two people who think the same, no two people who react the same. In other words, absorb what is useful and reject what is useless. You have to find your own path to the top of the mountain. What works for me may not work for you."

The danger of seeking your own path in Jeet Kune Do, say critics of the Concepts approach, is that a person may stray from the fundamental aspects of Bruce Lee's art. "The major issue with the Jeet Kune Do Concepts approach is that they delve into many other styles that eventually begins to change major principles in Jeet Kune Do," said Richard Torres. "A good example is the Jeet Kune Do principle of *Strong Side Forward*. Because of the influence of their boxing classes and Muay Thai classes, some Jeet Kune Do Concepts practitioners put their strong side back and put their weak side forward."

Richard Torres continued his comparison of the two approaches to Jeet Kune Do. "Another principle that has been changed is the idea of *range* as taught in Jeet Kune Do by Bruce Lee. In Original Jeet Kune Do, we teach *Long, Medium,* and *Close Range*. But in the Concepts approach, the ranges have been changed into *Kicking Range, Punching Range, Trapping Range,* and *Grappling Range*. Then the Concepts approach teaches that one can choose certain styles or disciplines in each individual range. So, they may teach French Savate in kicking range, Filipino Boxing in punching range, Wing Chun in trapping range, and Ju Jitsu in grappling range. Using styles in different ranges. This is totally not Jeet Kune Do. The art of Jeet Kune Do is not concerned with styles. We train the martial art tools."

New York-based "Original" Jeet Kune Do instructor Richard Torres.

Jeet Kune Do instructor Dwight Woods, of Florida, is wary of weighing in on the debate within Jeet Kune Do because he believes it is a false division and is not interest in perpetuating a rift. However, when asked to compare and contrast the two approaches, he offered his thoughts. "I'd say the singular 'advantage' of the Original Jeet Kune Do approach is that it can alleviate a challenge for some Concepts adherents by encouraging them to investigate whether they are indeed simplifying their technical base and not adding more and more techniques to that base. I point this out only because there does seem to be students and instructors from both camps who seem to think that 'technique collection' is a goal of martial arts cross-training. They have either forgotten, or were never aware of, the analysis, research, and development protocols of the Jeet Kune Do methodology. And I'd say that it's mostly the students and instructors who've come along after the mid-to-late 1990s and who possess a particular mindset. The problem with the Original Jeet Kune Do approach is that they can remain 'stuck' in their way of thinking and way of training if they choose to ignore the directive of *constant* analysis, research, and development. The obvious advantage of the Jeet Kune Do Concepts approach would be that they stay abreast of the current state of the arts."

Dwight Woods also believes the Jeet Kune Do Concepts approach is not about adding techniques from other styles so much as it is about enhancing the existing Jeet Kune Do techniques themselves. "I remember being at a Dan Inosanto seminar in Janesville, Wisconsin in the summer of 1988. Sifu Dan was demonstrating Jeet Kune Do trapping sequences and brought me up to assist and show the difference in 'penetration' between a Jeet Kune Do trap and a Pentjak Silat trap. He wanted to show that the Silat approach to trapping was more aggressive than the Jeet Kune Do, showcasing that adopting the Silat approach would be a way to enhance your Jeet Kune Do trapping. This is an example of using an element from another martial art system to *enhance* your Jeet Kune Do. Conversely, Sifu Inosanto *loosened* up the somewhat stiff, traditional Pentjak Silat approach to training by using Jeet Kune Do Kickboxing sequences as entry techniques to Silat finishing techniques. In essence, this is the Jeet Kune Do Concepts approach in action. Discovering something in another art which can enhance what you're already doing in Jeet Kune Do and adapting and/or adopting it by *JKDising* it!"

Florida-based Jeet Kune Do "Concepts" instructor Dwight Woods.

Burton Richardson believes that the ideas behind Jeet Kune Do extend beyond the martial art. "To make it simple, Jeet Kune Do Concepts is the idea of doing what you must to make yourself the best that you can be. Whether it is in martial arts, personal relationships, business, or other arts, the same concepts apply. Set a goal that is in line with your beliefs, find good teachers to coach you towards your goal, then concentrate on doing the work necessary to reach the goal. Test yourself periodically to gauge your progress, adjust your plan of action, then get back to work. That is the Jeet Kune Do Concept."

Larry Hartsell viewed the entire Jeet Kune Do debate as unnecessary. "Bruce would go to a point and then he would find something else and develop on it and go forward," Larry Hartsell explained. "That's why we believe in what we call the 'Concepts' of Jeet Kune Do. Some people still want to stay with the original Jeet Kune Do and that's fine, but Bruce was constantly changing. So, there's nothing wrong with Original Jeet Kune Do, and there is nothing wrong with Jeet Kune Do Concepts. It's just a matter of which way you want to go. That's why I'm still training."

Larry Hartsell demonstrating a technique on Leif T. Røbekk during a Jeet Kune Do seminar. (Photo courtesy of Leif T. Røbekk)

Over three decades have passed since the schism in Jeet Kune Do began, and it persists to this day – with no resolution in sight. Said Burton Richardson: "The Concepts versus Original Jeet Kune Do debate is like most conflicts where neither side is fully understood and neither side is totally wrong. The stereotypical Concepts group is big on research while the Original group emphasizes working on the basics that Bruce Lee practiced. The logical thing to do is to research to find more functional basics and train them until you are proficient with them against a resisting opponent. If the Jeet Kune Do Concept is to be the best that you can be, and we are talking about martial arts, then you must do what you can to be a competent fighter. For me, that means being functional in all the ranges, against one or many, armed or unarmed opponents, in a variety of environments. The training should be directed towards dealing with strong, aggressive, skillful opponents who are resisting 100%. You can train to look good against a partner who is cooperatively feeding a certain type of attack, but real fights are free. In a street situation, an assailant is going to resist you with everything he has. In order to be functional, one must practice the basics that have been proven to be effective in a training environment that is as close to all-out street combat as can be while maintaining safety. Bruce Lee advocated the use of protective gear, and I believe that this is a must if you want to progress realistically. You should spar with people from many different styles to see what you can learn from them. They will also point out your weaknesses so that you can work on strengthening these areas. If you don't test your skills under pressure and against full resistance, you will never develop true confidence in them."

Burton Richardson was not surprised by the division that occurred in Jeet Kune Do. "The divisiveness is a natural occurrence. Groups have grown, divided, and attacked one another since the beginning of civilization. On the one hand, I would rather that we just let everyone do their own thing. On the other hand, I think it is dangerous for instructors to teach ineffective fighting methods while leading their student to believe that he or she is invincible. In my experience, I have found that many of the methods that we used to practice are ineffective against the more advanced fighting strategies of today."

In any philosophical or religious movement there is always fragmentation in the way it is perpetuated. Take Christianity, for example. After the death of Jesus, the apostles went out and formed dif-

Lamar Davis conducting Jeet Kune Do class. (Photo courtesy of Lamar Davis)

ferent schools of Christian thought. Peter founded the Catholic faith in Rome, while James remained in Jerusalem and developed Jewish Christianity. The apostle Paul founded the Pauline Christianity movement, and the Jewish Christians were extremely opposed to Paul's interpretations. Martial arts are no different. When Aikido founder Morihei Uyeshiba passed away in 1969, his art began fragmenting, and now there are several different schools of Aikido thought – each with a different approach. Bruce Lee's contemporary Ed Parker, the grandmaster of the Kenpo system, passed away in the late 1980s, and now his system shows signs of fragmentation. It is an expected occurrence when the leader of a movement passes and the art or system is left in the hands of his disciples, each of whom will proceed based on their own personal experience and viewpoints. Therefore, the divisiveness of the two schools of Jeet Kune Do thought is a natural progression that follows a not entirely unexpected course. The truth is, they share more in common than they have in differences, not the least of which is their respect for and dedication to Bruce Lee.

For Jeet Kune Do, it really comes down to a matter of personal preference. Said Lamar Davis, a proponent of Original Jeet Kune Do: "I prefer Original Jeet Kune Do because of its simplicity and its raw street effectiveness. Of all the martial arts that I've experienced, nothing beats it for street effectiveness. I don't care what art

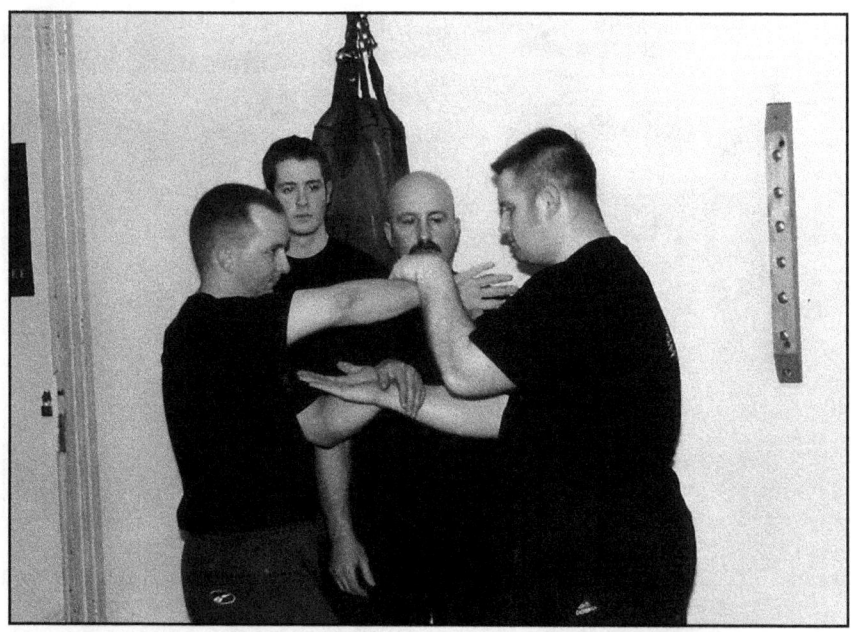
Students practicing sensitivity drills. (Photo courtesy of Martin O'Neill)

you compare it to; it is simple, direct, and non-classical. Everything is looked at from a practical standpoint. It emphasizes effective combat from all three ranges. It is very scientific, and everything is based on sound principles, theories, and strategies. Emphasis is on practical, no-nonsense targets such as the eyes, nose, throat, solar plexus, groin, knees, shins, and the instep. It is not for sport competition or tournament use. These are the things that make it work for me."

Standing in the middle of the road on the Jeet Kune Do debate is Patrick Strong, who offers a pretty good explanation for why Bruce Lee's different students think the way they do. "I like both sides. I really do, because the advantage of the Original Jeet Kune Do is that you've got a group of people that learned from Bruce. A lot these guys have stayed in the martial arts, and I'm sure many of them learned something from Bruce and, at the time they learned it, they may have caught it, or they may not have; but over the years, they caught it and they put it together. They picked up different little things from Bruce, and that's a body of knowledge. That body of knowledge is the closest thing you can get to Bruce's art. So, on the Original Jeet Kune Do side, you have these original tools that Bruce used, and what you try to do is get close to his original art. But what you have to remember is that he taught different people at different levels. He taught a lot of people different things. Certainly, his Seattle group was taught differently than his Oakland group; the Los Angeles group was taught differently than those two groups, but that was because his groups of students were all different. In Seattle, he didn't have any karate people to train. Everybody was a beginner, right from scratch. There were only a few of us that had done some boxing, and a couple of guys that had done some judo. So, he taught that group with more of the Wing Chun side to it. When he went to Oakland, he had some gung fu people there. James Lee was already a hard-hand gung fu guy. He got some other guys in there, but he trained them a great deal in the original stuff while he was also adding a lot of the boxing timing. When he came to Oakland, he had mostly Kenpo guys – guys that were already trained in the martial arts. But their martial art was based on rotation. Kenpo, Taekwondo, Shorin Ryu, all of these are based on rotation. Bruce's method is based on directional movement. So the guys that were from the Kenpo school come from the Kenpo home. Bruce's home was Wing Chun. The principles are directly opposed to one another. So, he wasn't trying to teach people Wing Chun, he was trying to teach them the principles of being able to free the body up to break away from the tradition, to get beyond the limitations of your art and call that Jeet Kune Do. But it doesn't mean that it was exactly what he was doing. In my opinion, Bruce had his personal art, and his personal art was quite a bit different than other people's art, because his core was Wing Chun. So now we come to the Jeet Kune Do Concepts. I don't see anything wrong with fighters taking Bruce's concepts and principles and applying them to their art (because that's basically what happened anyway) and then to go out and study other arts while applying Bruce's principles to them to make them work for you, and then you have your own expression. I do that myself, though I don't call it Concepts."

The Jun Fan Jeet Kune Do Nucleus

In January 1996, 13 of Bruce Lee's original students convened in Seattle, Washington for a historic summit. Brought together by Bruce Lee's widow, Linda Lee Cadwell, the purpose of the meeting was to try to unify the Jeet Kune Do community and provide focus and direction for Bruce Lee's martial art. Because of the rampant abuse of the name "Jeet Kune Do" by fraudulent teachers, it was decided that the martial art techniques and practices as advocated

In January 1996, 13 of Bruce Lee's original students convened in Seattle, Washington for a historic summit. (Photo courtesy of Richard Torres)

by Bruce Lee in his lifetime would thereafter be called Jun Fan Jeet Kune Do (Jun Fan being Bruce Lee's birth name). The name was then trademarked, protecting it from unauthorized infringement.

The most important development to come from the Seattle meeting was the formation of the Jun Fan Jeet Kune Do Nucleus, an organization whose stated purpose was to "promote understanding through providing the means for those seeking information about the art of Bruce Lee." It was a historical and educational organization designed to preserve the knowledge that Bruce Lee passed on to his students and share it with the world.

"The Nucleus is a non-profit organization," said founding member Steve Golden. "We members are doing this because we care. All proceeds are used to continue the dissemination of Bruce Lee's teaching. We do not get paid for these seminars or for our participation in the Nucleus."

"The Nucleus has nothing at all to say about Jeet Kune Do," added Golden. "It specifically addresses Jun Fan Jeet Kune Do only. Jeet Kune Do has taken on the definition, over the years, of however people feel like defining it."

Not only did the new organization serve as a repository of knowledge on Bruce Lee and Jun Fan Jeet Kune Do, it was a means by which a person interested in learning the art of Jun Fan Jeet Kune Do could find or verify an instructor. Though it did not certify instructors, the Jun Fan Jeet Kune Do Nucleus did recognize qualified instructors who studied under original members of the Nucleus.

Said Steve Golden: "The Nucleus does not decide what Jun Fan Jeet Kune Do is. Bruce Lee decided that. We want people to know what he was teaching and speak up if someone misrepresents his teaching. Opinions of where Bruce might have gone if he had lived longer is beyond our scope, and anyone is free to surmise whatever they want. My opinion is that he would not have suddenly changed his philosophy because some new art got 'popular'."

Lamar Davis, who studied under several of the Nucleus' founding members, was relieved to hear that the action was happening. Davis recognized the problem some years earlier, forming his own organization to maintain the integrity of Bruce Lee's art. He viewed the formation of the Jun Fan Jeet Kune Do Nucleus as better late than never. "I have been extremely excited by the forming of the Jun Fan Jeet Kune Do Nucleus, and I joined the Jun Fan Jeet Kune Do Association as soon as general membership was available. I am proud to be a member of such a distinguished group, and I will continue to support their efforts."

Unfortunately, though Dan Inosanto was a part of the founding of the Nucleus, he chose to leave the organization after the first meeting. Inosanto felt he could better perpetuate his teacher Bruce Lee's art and stay true to his commitment to Lee by continuing his Concepts approach.

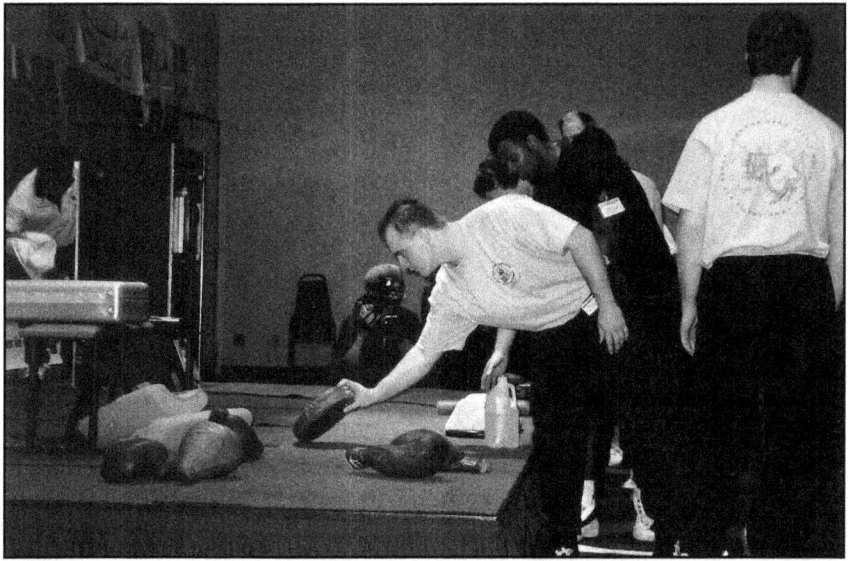

At the 2000 Bruce Lee Educational Foundation conference in Las Vegas, participants viewed and handled Bruce Lee's training equipment. (Author's archives)

The Jun Fan Jeet Kune Do Nucleus conferences gave fans and martial artists an opportunity to meet family, friends, and students of Bruce Lee. (Author's archives)

"He (Inosanto) wanted to do more of his own thing, the Filipino martial arts, which he is Filipino," Larry Hartsell said. Soon after Inosanto left, Hartsell followed, out of respect and love for his teacher, and because he, too, felt that the Concepts approach was the best path for him. It was a decision that was respected by most of the Nucleus members, including Bruce Lee's widow, Linda Lee Cadwell. Wrote Mrs. Cadwell: "It is the intent of the Nucleus to work along parallel paths rather than at cross purposes with others who are expressing their respect for Bruce in their own way. We do not choose to take part in 'separative nonsenses,' as Bruce said, or to create a rival organization claiming to possess the 'truth' to the exclusion of all others. We seek only to be a repository of information, a starting point for the martial artist beginning his process of self-discovery."

The Jun Fan Jeet Kune Do Nucleus published a newsletter and a magazine during the six-year existence of the organization. In its third year, it rebranded itself the Bruce Lee Educational Foundation in order to broaden its appeal beyond the martial arts aspect of Bruce Lee's life. The Nucleus also hosted five martial arts conferences during its short existence. The first three were in places of historical interest regarding Bruce Lee: Los Angeles, Oakland, and Seattle. The final two were in Las Vegas and Holland. The conferences were a unique opportunity to learn from a group of Bruce Lee's friends, family, and students in one central place.

Facing mounting financial pressures and the loss of support of the Lee family, the Jun Fan Jeet Kune Do Nucleus/Bruce Lee Educational Foundation dissolved in 2002.

The Fans

Perhaps the most surprising aspect of the Bruce Lee legacy is the effect he has on fans who never even knew him. From the die-hard collectors who dedicate a good part of their lives to accumulating Bruce Lee memorabilia, to the fans who take Lee's example of excellence and apply it to their lives, these people are, in their own way, keeping Bruce Lee alive.

"Although I never met him, Bruce has been a positive role model in my life and has impressed me deeply," said *Jeff Chinn,* a Bruce Lee memorabilia collector from Daly City, California. Chinn has one of the most extensive Bruce Lee memorabilia collections in the world. "He was the first person I've ever heard say that he was proud to be Chinese. Bruce, more than anyone, showed me how a Chinese could be just as good as anyone else, if not better. In fact, some of my favorite scenes from his movies are the ones in which Bruce fought racism."

Over the years, collector Jeff Chinn amassed one of the largest Bruce Lee memorabilia collections in the world. (Photo courtesy of Jeff Chinn)

Chinn's connection to Bruce Lee goes all the way back to his birth. "I was born on February 22, 1961, in San Francisco, California. The hospital of my birth is The Chinese Hospital on Jackson Street – the very same hospital in which Bruce Lee was born.

"My very first exposure to Bruce Lee was watching him as Kato on the ABC TV series *The Green Hornet* in 1966. Since I was only five years old at the time, I only knew him as Kato and not as Bruce Lee. I remember that my entire family watched this TV show every Friday night and it was very special to all of us. Chinese were practically invisible on TV in those days (even now), and we always noticed whenever a Chinese appeared on the screen. But it was even more special watching Kato, because he was not the usual stereotypical weak "Ahh So" Chinese that were so common back then. For once (or one entire TV season), we felt good after watching 'one of us' on TV. The two most memorable things about Kato from 33 years ago were his blinding speed and his intensity (those battle cries were awesome!).

"Six years later, in 1972, was the beginning of the *kung fu craze*, and I was totally swept up by it. I watched the TV series *Kung Fu* every single week and was totally engrossed with anything about the martial arts. I was at the impressionable age of 11. I would go to the bookstores and buy whatever books that were available. That year, a neighborhood friend gave me a magazine that he thought I would like to have. The magazine was *New Martial Arts Hero* issue number 72 and had this skinny but muscular Chinese guy on the cover. My friend kept emphasizing how this Chinese guy named Bruce Lee was so incredible, and that I should try to watch one of his movies that was playing in Chinatown. When I asked him if Bruce Lee was as good as David Carradine (the star of the *Kung Fu* television series), my friend burst out laughing! Unfortunately, my dad would not take me to any movie playing in Chinatown because he said the theaters were too dirty. In the meantime, I would occasionally purchase more magazines with Bruce on the cover during my weekly trips to Chinatown. Although I had not seen one of his movies yet, Bruce looked pretty good to me. It wouldn't be until the following year that I would see my first Bruce Lee movie when *The Big Boss* was dubbed and released as *Fists of Fury* in a 'clean' American theater."

The Big Boss and Bruce Lee did not disappoint Chinn in the least. "Watching *The Big Boss* was an unforgettable experience for me and totally changed my life. I remember that Bruce was not only incredibly fast, strong and agile, but that he was very entertaining and drove everyone in the theater into a frenzy! The magnificent way he could control his body made my jaw drop! I've never seen anyone do what he did on the screen. Bruce was for real! I walked

Jeff Chinn poses proudly in the blue silk Chinese gung fu suit that Bruce Lee wore in Enter the Dragon, *the most cherished piece from Chinn's Bruce Lee collection. Chinn bought it at auction in 1993 for $8,000.* (Photo courtesy of Jeff Chinn)

out of the theater feeling 10 feet tall and so proud to be Chinese! I definitely wanted to be like my hero! Bruce touched me on a deep emotional level. After the movie, my dad told me that Bruce Lee was the same person who played Kato on the TV series. I was surprised when I heard this, but when he told me that I was also born in the same hospital as Bruce, I almost fainted!"

Bruce Lee's impact on Jeff Chinn is similar to the experiences of many of Lee's fans. Bruce Lee wanted to give the world a Chinese hero, and he was very successful in achieving his goal. For Chinese and Chinese Americans, Lee was a validation of their heritage. For other races and minority groups, Bruce Lee was equally inspiring.

For Jeff Chinn, *The Big Boss* cemented his lifelong obsession with Bruce Lee. "Bruce Lee became my hero and role model. I wanted to be just like him and learn as much as I could about him. I would get a thrill just to see his picture."

Jeff Chinn particularly recalls a piece of Bruce Lee memorabilia he acquired in 1975. "It was the first time that I ordered a Bruce Lee item through the mail, a handmade flipbook from *Enter the Dragon*. I saw it advertised in the *Comics Buyer's Guide*. The handmade flipbook featured the famous scene of Bruce Lee swinging his nunchucks. Since it was my very first Bruce Lee flipbook, I must have flipped it over a thousand times! Fast, slow, forward, *and* backward. I had hours upon hours of enjoyment with the only available 'footage' of Bruce Lee at home!"

That flipbook was just one of many pieces of memorabilia that comprise Jeff Chinn's collection. "The first couple of years of collecting mainly consisted of items from my weekly visits to Chinatown," said Chinn. "Unlike today, San Francisco Chinatown was a gold mine of Bruce Lee memorabilia in the early seventies. Unfortunately for me, I only got 75 cents a week for allowance, which was only good for one magazine a week. Sometimes, when I look at some sentimental items, I think back and relive the magical times in the darkened movie theaters when I saw Bruce Lee movies for the first time. The special memories of everyone cheering and going crazy over the heroics of Bruce Lee were a once in a lifetime experience."

Although he wanted to learn gung fu, financial reasons prevented Jeff Chinn from taking gung fu lessons in his youth. Chinn found other ways to emulate his hero. "I could not afford to take gung fu lessons as a young teen, so I did the next best thing in trying to be like Bruce by exercising. I ran, lifted weights, and did calisthenics to get my body to look like Bruce's. I never stopped and continue

Jeff Chinn with his wife Julie at the Jun Fan Jeet Kune Do Third Annual Conference in Seattle in 1999.

to keep in shape in my adult life. I also have Bruce to thank for something I am very proud of. I currently hold the Skyline College Fitness Academy record, which is a point system test consisting of push-ups, pull-ups, sit-ups, flexibility, vertical jump, 60-yard dash and two-mile run. I set the record in 1981 and to this day it has not been close to being broken."

Jeff Chinn continues to collect, and he gained his own fame for his collection of Bruce Lee memorabilia. "I've amassed one of the world's largest collections. I don't really collect like crazy anymore and mainly concentrate on vintage items from the kung fu craze of 1972-75. Running out of room! My focus now is to use my collection to share and teach Bruce Lee's important life and legacy to others. I do this by loaning my collection to museums throughout the world and having visitors come to my personal museum, *The Bruce Lee Room*. My museum has been visited by fans from all over the world as well as friends and students of Bruce Lee. Past special guests include Bruce Lee students Taky Kimura, Ted Wong, George Lee, Allen Joe, Steve Golden, Pete Jacobs, Chris Kent, and, of course, Bruce Lee's widow, Linda Lee Cadwell."

Jeff Chinn with Bruce Lee's daughter, Shannon Lee, at the the grand opening of the Academy Museum of Motion Pictures in Los Angeles for the Bruce Lee exhibit (2021). (Photo courtesy of Jeff Chinn)

As his reputation grew, Jeff Chinn became a prominent presence in the martial arts media. "I wrote articles and a bi-monthly column on Bruce Lee for *Inside Kung Fu* magazine. I've also appeared in many other magazines, books, and newspapers as well as several TV shows on the subject of my collection and Bruce Lee. I feel like one of the luckiest fans in the world."

Among the thousands of items Chinn has collected, there is one that is most special to him. "The most cherished piece in my entire collection is the actual blue-silk Chinese gung fu suit Bruce Lee wore in *Enter the Dragon*. I bought it at an auction, which sold items that were stored by Linda Lee after Bruce's death. As a fan and collector, Bruce's films mean the most to me, and I had always wished that I could own something he wore or used in one of them. One of my biggest thrills was when I tried on the suit, and it fit me perfectly! My wife took plenty of pictures while I posed for the camera as proud as I could be. Every time I see *Enter the Dragon* and look at the famous scenes of Bruce wearing the blue suit, I still get a nice tingle knowing that I'm the owner of the suit."

Jeff Chinn is proud when he has the opportunity to share the gung fu suit with the public. "My *Enter the Dragon* gung fu suit was

A sign advertising the "We Are Bruce Lee: Under the Sky, One Family" exhibit at the Chinese Historical Society of America's museum in San Francisco. Exhibit tour guide Jeff Chinn is prominently featured on the advertisement alongside Bruce Lee. (Photo courtesy of Jeff Chinn)

on display at the grand opening of the Academy Museum of Motion Pictures in Los Angeles for the Bruce Lee exhibit (2021). Shannon Lee and I loaned items for the Asian American section of the museum. A beautiful display honoring Bruce Lee at such a prestigious museum! A proud moment for me indeed honoring the legacy of Bruce Lee and Asian American representation in Hollywood! My wife and I visited the museum several times. I would spend most of my time at the Bruce Lee exhibit and gave tours as an unofficial docent. This special exhibit lasted for around one and a half years.

Now retired from his career with the United States Postal Service, Jeff Chinn donates his time to the Chinese Historical Society of America, where he is the chief loaner of artifacts and main docent tour guide of their museum's *We are Bruce Lee: Under the Sky, One Family exhibition*. In this position, Chinn is able to share his lifetime of scholarship on Bruce Lee with the public, as well as pieces from his own collection. "As the main docent tour guide for our *We Are Bruce Lee* exhibition, I have the privilege of sharing his life, legacy and also a little bit about myself. I truly enjoy the opportunity to meet visitors from all around the world."

Martial artist and professional sculptor Boyd Thomas. (Author's archives)

Though not a collector of Bruce Lee memorabilia, martial artist and professional sculptor *Boyd Thomas* was definitely influenced by Bruce Lee. Unlike some, Thomas was already in the martial arts when he discovered Lee. A student of Taekwondo and Shotokan Karate, Thomas' instructors were a "Who's Who" of the "Texas Blood-N-Guts Karate" period: Glen Dicus, Tim Kirby, Allen Steen, Dennis Gotcher, and *Black Belt* Hall of Fame members Demetrius "The Greek" Havanas, Roy Kurban, and Ray McCallum.

Boyd Thomas' first exposure to Bruce Lee came in 1972. *"The Big Boss* came out, and I went to the drive-in to see that," said Thomas. "It was a real spark of adrenaline, because I was thinking, *Man! Can anybody ever get that good, you know? Is it just a film, or is there actually someone who can fight like that?* I had already been in martial arts for four years and started tournament fighting the year before. I thought about all the martial artists that I had ever met, and then to see someone like that – it was awesome!"

Bruce Lee's effect on Thomas was profound and immediate. "I went into the Bruce Lee craze, mimicking the kicking, punching, and the yelling. *The whole bit.* I got lost in that for about a year, until I noticed all these different people at tournaments trying to copy his movements. I had a realization: I may not be able to master it to that point but, on the personal side, I would strive to be as good as

I could be. So, I concentrated on my own attributes and aptitudes, and developed my own way of fighting. I developed a sidekick that became very well respected in the Texas tournament circuit. I could drop anybody with that sidekick. It was unstoppable."

One thing Boyd Thomas did retain from watching Bruce Lee was the concept of drawing the opponent. "Watching Bruce Lee made me conscious of the ability to trick the opponent into getting into the position I wanted him in; how to fake an opening and set up people for a technique."

In high school at the time, Thomas would combine his artistic talent and his passion for Bruce Lee by making money painting pictures of Lee for people who knew him. He gained quite a reputation for his work. It also helped him develop his skills as an artist. "I hadn't really gotten into drawing people before I developed my interest in Bruce Lee. But drawing and painting all those pictures of Lee helped me to refine and improve my skill at human anatomy, you know, the physique and all."

Thomas said that, being black, Bruce Lee was also an inspiration to himself and other black men as a symbol of a strong minority figure. "Everybody I knew was fascinated with the guy. When you mentioned his name, friends got excited. They respected him."

"Bruce had a lot going for him, but, at the same time, he dealt with *racism*. There is still racism in the world today, and, like Bruce, there may have been some opportunities that I have missed out on because of my race. But Bruce Lee never let that get him down, and he never let it stop him. I feel the same way. Also, like Bruce, I refuse to see the world and its people in colors. I choose my friends for their character and their intelligence, not for their skin. And you know what? I find, with that attitude, people tend not to see me in terms of color."

Boyd Thomas demonstrating kicking to his student. (Author's archives)

Boyd Thomas at work on one of his sculpting projects. (Courtesy of Boyd Thomas)

Boyd Thomas took Bruce Lee's example to heart and pursued his own dreams, taking his talent as an artist and making it a profession. For most of his career, Thomas worked as a commercial sculptor. "Bruce made me want to go beyond being a martial artist and to try to be the best that I could be at whatever I was doing," said Boyd Thomas. "The type of drive that Bruce Lee had (to produce what he produced over the years), I would say, is an inspiration to me as an artist."

Bruce Lee collector Robert Blakeman (Photo courtesy of Darin Waugh)

Ohio resident *Robert Blakeman* collected Bruce Lee memorabilia beginning in 1973, shortly after Lee died and *Enter the Dragon* was released. "The first thing I ever collected was a newspaper clipping out of the local *Columbus Dispatch*," he said.

"I knew who he was because he was 'Kato' in *The Green Hornet* in 1966," continued Blakeman. "I was a big fan of the Green Hornet and especially Kato. I remember at the grocery store, I was probably eight or nine, I saw Kato on the cover of *TV Guide*. My mother bought it for me. I lost it, but when I started collecting, someone gave me another copy of it."

Over the years, Blakeman collected thousands of different items. "I have about everything you could think of: books, magazines, cups, cans, posters, t-shirts, and statues. Probably the most prized possession I own is a letter Bruce wrote to a fan when he was on *The Green Hornet*. It's on his stationary and is signed, in English and in Chinese, *The Little Dragon*."

Blakeman is quick to explain his fascination with Bruce Lee. "I think he represents perfection in an individual. That's probably why I've been intrigued so long with him.

"He was on the *Longstreet* television show, and I remember watching it the very first time it aired. That (the episode titled "Way of the Intercepting Fist") really impressed me because I didn't understand his philosophy until then. Being an enthusiastic fan, I came to understand that this was a person of great insight."

To share his love of Bruce Lee with others, Blakeman spearheaded an annual memorial to Bruce Lee in Columbus. *Bruce Lee Eve,* as it was called, was an event he started in 1983 to celebrate the life of Bruce Lee as well as educate people on the different dimensions of his character. Blakeman put on display parts of his Bruce Lee memorabilia collection, which included over 4,000 magazines and 10,000 photographs of Lee.

Blakeman fondly remembers his first Bruce Lee Eve. "It was the 10th anniversary of Bruce Lee's death, and I couldn't find anything recognizing the importance of his passing. Bruce Lee's face was not on any magazine. Nothing. I thought to myself, '*This is ridiculous. It's the 10th anniversary of his death and nothing's going on.*' So, I decided to have a Bruce Lee Eve on July 20, 1983. I really didn't know what I was doing. I had it at my house. I sent out a bunch of press releases. *The Columbus Dispatch* did an article on it, and the 11 o'clock news came to cover the story. It was exciting because I felt like Bruce was being remembered. So that was an incentive for me to keep doing it every year.

"In 1986, I decided to open it up to the public. I had it at the

Robert Blakeman with Vicki Hecker holding the letter from Bruce Lee at the 1986 Bruce Lee Eve event. Hecker stood in line for 40 minutes at the Roxy Theatre for the opportunity to show Blakeman the letter. (Image courtesy of Robert Blakeman)

Robert Blakeman with Richard Torres at the 1987 Bruce Lee Eve. (Photo courtesy of Darin Waugh)

Roxy Theater. *USA Today* put it in their 'Lifeline' column and it was a sellout. It was a really, really neat event, and that was when I met Vicki Hecker, who gave me the hand-written letter Bruce Lee wrote to her when she was little. She asked me to authenticate it for her, and when she handed me the letter, I about fell down!" Blakeman laughed. "I said, *'That's uh, that's uh, that's authentic!'"* The next year, Hecker decided to give the letter to Blakeman. Vicki Hecker felt that Blakeman would take good care of it, and she wanted the letter to be seen and appreciated.

The annual Bruce Lee Eve event became popular among Bruce Lee fans in Columbus and abroad, even spawning a small fan club called A.B.L.E (Associates of Bruce Lee Eve). Held in the basement of his home for the first three years of its existence, the growing attendance forced Robert Blakeman to seek a new venue in 1986. Bruce Lee Eve was held at a number of locations over the next decade, including the Roxy and Drexel Theaters. Beginning in 1998, the Video Central rental store on Livingston Avenue became the home of Bruce Lee Eve. "At Video Central, I have an entire room for the Bruce Lee exhibit, so I am able to display a lot of good stuff," said Blakeman.

The first Bruce Lee Eve held at Video Central surprised the rental store's staff. "Video Central said there were more than 300

Columbus Dispatch *article on the 1993 Bruce Lee Eve.* (Image courtesy of Robert Blakeman)

people who came to the event over a four-hour period. The line would go all through the store and into the Bruce Lee room. It was exciting. There was a local wushu (kung fu) school that performed a lion's dance, and they did an exceptional job. It was very beautiful. I had a Bruce Lee photo tribute with candles and incense in the Bruce Lee Eve room and the 'lion' bowed several times at the photograph. They also did a martial arts demonstration."

Many of the people who attended the event were surprised by what they found out about Bruce Lee. "A lot of people couldn't believe there was so much in one person. So many times, they could not believe there was so much information and memorabilia. The older people would say, *'Hey, I remember that poster! I used to have it in my bedroom!'* The younger guests would see things they had never seen before.

"I like to work really hard on the displays. It's very difficult to do. I would like to have a museum. That has always been my goal, that it looks classy, and it's presented well. So, I try to make it classy, but it looks a little overwhelming because there is so much stuff."

Blakeman had particularly fond memories of the 1987 Bruce Lee Eve. That year, Bruce Lee student Larry Hartsell attended the celebration. "It was just a thrill! He demonstrated Bruce's One-Inch Punch. He was there, not for money, but out of his heart, which was just extraordinary! He was simply one of the nicest people I have ever met. He was, like Bruce Lee, a 'genuine' person. Sometimes it is hard to meet people in the martial arts who are genuine."

Flyer for what turned out to be Robert Blakeman's final Bruce Lee Eve event. (Flyer courtesy of Robert Blakeman)

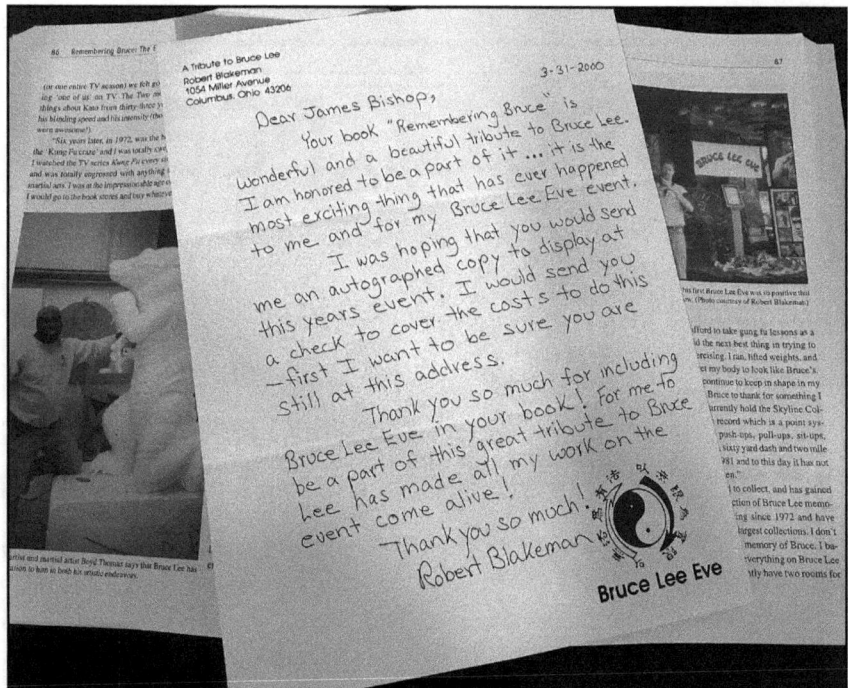

Robert Blakeman was honored to be featured in the 1999 edition of this book. (Author's archives)

When this book was published as *Remembering Bruce* in 1999, it represented the largest exposure that Robert Blakeman's lifelong dedication to Bruce Lee was ever given. Blakeman, who humbly continued his local tradition of honoring Bruce Lee for many years, was overjoyed with the recognition. "Your book *Remembering Bruce* is wonderful and a beautiful tribute to Bruce Lee," he wrote in a letter to this author after receiving the book. "I am honored to be a part of it. It is the most exciting thing that has ever happened to me and for my Bruce Lee Eve event." Blakeman proudly displayed a copy of *Remembering Bruce* at his 2000 Bruce Lee Eve. He held a drawing for the book and a winner was able to go home with it.

The 2000 Bruce Lee Eve was held at Video Central on July 20th; not coincidentally, the 27th anniversary of the death of Bruce Lee. "This year, I estimated close to 300 people attended over the four-hour event," said Blakeman. "We had martial arts demos and a Chinese Lion dance by the Wah Lum Kung Fu and Tai Chi of USA school. Many of these people wore white to honor Bruce Lee. In addition to my Bruce Lee collection, there were flowers, dragons, and incense that filled the entire place in his memory."

As always, Robert Blakeman's satisfaction from his Bruce Lee Eve events came from the knowledge that he was keeping Lee's memory alive. "As I talked to the guests," he said, "there is always a wonderful feeling of respect and awe of Bruce Lee's accomplishments during his lifetime."

The July 2000 Bruce Lee Eve event would turn out to be Robert Blakeman's last. In October, Blakeman suffered the first of a series of strokes. He suffered two more strokes over the next several months before passing away on July 11, 2001, at the age of 45.

"You know, Robert never made a nickel from Bruce Lee Eve," said his close friend, Darin Waugh. "Even when we held the event at the theater, he never got a piece of the admission, and he never tried to sell memorabilia or anything. He did it purely for his admiration for Bruce Lee and the pleasure he received for doing his part to keep Bruce's memory alive."

Robert Blakeman, who was gay, did not share a lot about his personal life with others. Outside of his public efforts to honor Bruce Lee, Blakeman was a very private man. His funeral was a subdued affair attended by his partner, Mickey Prince, Blakeman's immediate family, and a small group of friends.

Robert Blakeman (Photo courtesy of Darin Waugh)

"My wife and I attended Robert's funeral service, and, in many ways, it was truly sad," said Darin Waugh. "No friends or family stood up to say a few words about Robert. The minister, who obviously didn't know Robert, seemed more interested in saving souls than in talking about the human being laying in the casket. I was tempted to stand up and say something, but I knew I was probably the only one there who could truly understand what Robert's passion, in terms of Bruce Lee, *really* meant."

Robert Blakeman and his friend, Darin Waugh. (Photo courtesy of Darin Waugh)

After Robert Blakeman's death, Mickey Prince assumed ownership of his partner's Bruce Lee memorabilia collection – believed to be among the largest Bruce Lee collections in the world. Prince offered the collection to Darin Waugh, but Waugh was unable to purchase it at the time. "His partner asked me if I wanted to buy it for $10,000," said Waugh, "but I had just bought a house."

When Mickey Prince died six months after the death of Robert Blakeman, Blakeman's Bruce Lee memorabilia collection was bequeathed to Ohio Grandmaster Joon P. Choi, Blakeman's childhood Taekwondo instructor. Grandmaster Choi dutifully cared for the collection until his own death in 2021. The current status of Robert Blakeman's Bruce Lee memorabilia collection, where it is or whether it remains intact at all, is unknown.

"Newer collectors probably haven't heard too much about Norman Borine and Robert Blakeman, but they were the pioneers," said John Negron, a Bruce Lee collector. "They were the ones who opened the doors for all of us, who inspired us to collect. It would be interesting, if he were alive, to see how much he progressed."

"As long as we remember him, Bruce Lee lives," Robert Blakeman told the attendees at the 1986 Bruce Lee Eve. Like Bruce Lee, Robert Blakeman inspired a lot of people in his short life, and so long as the Bruce Lee fandom remembers him, Blakeman will continue to live as well.

Jon Benn was unique in that he was not only a fan of Bruce Lee but also his co-star in the movie *Way of the Dragon*. They came to know each other after Lee returned to Hong Kong.

"Bruce and I were both from San Francisco," said Benn. "He was San Francisco street smart and spoke perfect English and not so perfect Cantonese. He was great to work with as he was always joking and having fun. He loved to show off, as he knew that he was the best. Bruce never stopped moving and was always punching and kicking – even on the set waiting for the lights to change, etc. He sometimes kicked the ash off my cigar without moving the cigar...he was that accurate. He got along well with everyone, but once the camera was on, he was very serious and got what he wanted."

Way of the Dragon co-star and self-professed Bruce Lee fan, Jon Benn.

In June of 1998, Benn rebranded his five-year-old Hong Kong restaurant as the *Bruce Lee Café and Museum*. "The sad thing is that Bruce was Hong Kong's number one son," he said. "He put Hong Kong on the map when few knew what or where it was. For 25 years there was no memorial, no statue, no plaque...nothing. Tens of thousands of his fans came looking for something and left disappointed. Even though there is a large fan club here of some 900 members, neither they nor the government did anything. I finally came along and changed my place into the Bruce Lee Cafe and Museum. Still, neither the government nor the fan club did anything to support me, as I am a round eye and they were upset that I, not

At the Bruce Lee Café and Museum, guests could dine on such offerings as the "Fish of Fury", "Flying Kick Chicken", and the "Kung Fu Curry" of the day. (Photo courtesy of Jon Benn)

them, finally did something."

Benn's Bruce Lee Café and Museum became well known to Bruce Lee fans. "We had all of his original film posters and lobby cards on display," he said, "plus his nunchakus that he gave me after the movie, and his training shin guards. Also, his black gung fu jacket and a pair of shoes. This plus many photos and other memorabilia. Many hundreds of his fans visited and all were impressed. They took many pictures, and I signed many autographs and answered all their questions."

Benn ran the Bruce Lee Café and Museum until 2001. According to him, over 20,000 fans visited the restaurant during the three years of its existence. So many people sought out the Bruce Lee Café and Museum, the Hong Kong government was compelled to make Jon Benn a goodwill ambassador for the city. Despite this, he made the difficult decision to close the Bruce Lee Café and Museum after the rising cost of the property lease no longer made the venture profitable.

John Benn appeared in his last two movies, *The Way of the Spur* and *The Man with the Iron Fists,* in 2012. Benn retired to Louisville, Kentucky where he passed away on December 9, 2018, at the age of 83.

Dublin native *Joe Hanley*, like Jon Benn, is an actor with a lifelong interest in all things Bruce Lee. As an Irish boy growing up in 1970s, Hanley was struck by Lee's dynamism and the way the little dragon seemed to leap off the screen and speak directly to him.

"I remember I was a kid," said Hanley, recalling the moment when he first became aware of Bruce Lee. "It was the mid-to-late seventies. My brother was into Bruce Lee when Lee was sweeping Ireland and the UK; you know, 1974-1976, around that time, because I don't think those films premiered over here until six months or more after they premiered in the states. Yeah, Bruce Lee was introduced, and I remember that book, which I still have, titled *Bruce Lee: King of Kung Fu*. It was written in '74 and is one of the first ones that came out, and I think it is still one of the best. But my brother had that book, and I remember looking through it."

Actor and devoted Bruce Lee fan, Joe Hanley. (Photo courtesy of Joe Hanley)

Joe Hanley grew up in the working-class neighborhood of Cabra, a suburb on the northside of Dublin, where disagreements were often resolved with fists. He never knew his father as a child, and Hanley's relationship with his mother would sometimes be difficult. Despite sharing a house with his three brothers, the absence of a father had a profound effect on the young boy, and he yearned for a father figure and role model.

Hanley, a gifted artist, demonstrated his talent for drawing early in his life. "As far back as I can remember, I've always drawn," he said. "Since a baby, it was a given. My mother was a bit indifferent to it; perhaps she was too busy. I suppose when I was six or seven years old, I knew something was up by the reaction of people outside of the home who saw my artwork."

Art became a creative outlet and a way to fill the time in his somewhat isolated life. "I had three brothers and a sister, but they were much older than me by at least 10 years," said Hanley. "They were adults and had their own lives, and my mother was usually working. I often spent that time alone, and I think that's why I started to draw."

Hanley vividly remembered the moment "Bruce Lee Mania" exploded in his community. "So, it was the mid-seventies, and, like the Carl Douglas song, everybody was kung fu fighting; the craze just swept the world," he said. "It definitely swept Ireland and especially where I come from. I remember all the kids around the street corner were all going to see Bruce Lee in a double-bill of *The Big Boss* and *Fist of Fury;* they asked me if I was coming along, but I didn't want to go. I said no, but I became curious, though, as they were going all week. They went every day and, eventually, around mid-week, I went along. And that was it. I mean, they all loved it, and they all came out and start jumping around imitating Bruce Lee's moves."

The excitement that Joe Hanley felt when Bruce Lee made his debut on screen was immediate and potent. "I was literally floored when I first saw Bruce Lee. I mean, it's true what they say – he had a magnetism that leapt off the screen and especially, of course, when he fought. I was 12 or nearly 13 at the time and getting bullied a lot where I grew up, like a lot of boys. Every underdog, they always think of being like Bruce Lee, kicking ass. I became more obsessive about Bruce Lee than the other guys around the street. And it wasn't just the fighting; I looked up to him."

Hanley recalled going to the cinema and watching Bruce Lee films over and over again. "Bruce Lee was in the theaters for six months straight; they'd go away then come back again. They just showed those films all day every day. Of course, the guys – the young kids – they obsessed over that for a while and then they moved on to something else. But I just kept going back to the movies again and again. I'd go in for the noon show and I would stay until the last showing; I'd watch three of them back-to-back. I'd come home and my mother would say *'Where the hell were you?'* I'd say, *'I was watching Bruce Lee.'* She couldn't understand the interest. She would mimic Bruce Lee. *'Bruce Lee, that's all you do!*

Wataah!' I just became obsessed with it, you know. There was one time I went to see *Enter the Dragon* and *Easy Rider* on a double bill – which was a crazy film for a 13-year-old to go see – and I sat through that just to watch *Enter the Dragon*. But usually it was *The Big Boss, Fist of Fury,* and *Way of the Dragon*. The fight scenes were great, but even *The Big Boss* – which has its charm – you can see was made for about $50. Now you look back and go, *'That was really hokey.'* You could say they all are, but I think *Fist of Fury* is my favorite."

Bruce Lee's martial arts movies in the 1970s led to many people seeking martial arts instruction, and Joe Hanley was no different. "Within a week or two, I was looking for kung fu classes," he said. "I didn't know anyone who trained. I didn't know anyone in the in martial arts, obviously. I mean, just the kids around the corner who were all going around thinking that they were Bruce. I started looking through the Golden Pages telephone directory for karate or kung fu schools and found one. So, I got the address, and I went down to them within a week or two and signed up."

Hanley signed up for classes at the Glasnevin Kenpo Karate Club, where instructor Ambrose Maloney taught as a representative of Ed Parker's American Kenpo system. "It just happened to be the nearest school to me," he said, looking back on that moment. "You know, I don't think, at the time, there were any kung fu schools in Ireland. Maybe there was, but I didn't know of it. I just wanted to join and get my suit, *my gi,* and start training. I just became obsessed with it. I became very good at it, pretty quickly."

Joe Hanley found he had a natural aptitude for fighting. "I think in a few weeks, maybe a month, I earned my yellow belt, and then I just rose through the ranks. Within three years or so, I was European Junior Champion. Junior because I was in the under 21 category, even though I was 16. I fought a guy in the Final in Dusseldorf who I think was 20 or 21, who was a lot bigger than me and was older, but that's the guy I beat for the title. He was European Kenpo karate champion and I said, *Yeah, I want that.* So, that's how I got started in it."

Inspired by Bruce Lee, Hanley trained hard to become the best that he could be at martial arts. "I mean, man, I'm gonna tell you about the training. I was there every Tuesday, Thursday, and Sunday. I became so obsessed, I took to judo, because I was reading a lot about Bruce Lee then, about his multi-disciplinary approach to fighting. And even then, I knew that the grappling wasn't in the Ken-

Kenpo stylist Joe Hanley became Junior European Champion in 1983. (Photo courtesy of Joe Hanley)

po. I remember getting into a few scraps on the street, because, I mean, guys would come up to me and go, *Joey, I hear you're doing karate* – and I'm only 14 or whatever. And they'd go, *'Do you need a license, you know, to show people before you fight? That you have a license, like a badge or card?'* And, of course, some guys would come down and challenge me and say, *'Come on, show me your karate.'* And I'd say, *'I don't want to'* and all that, but sometimes you had to fight. I remember one guy was older, and I was pretty fast. I caught him and all that. But then he grabbed me and got me down on the ground. I was kind of lost, you know, and we just ended up wrestling like a normal street fight, just trying to get headlocks, and so I realized that there was a deficiency in the Kenpo thing. So, I got into the Judo on the days that I wasn't training down at the club. I went to Finglas Judo, which was about two or three miles from my Kenpo school. And then, as I say, I got more into reading about Bruce Lee, and when I got the *Tao of Jeet Kune Do* and read about all the different disciplines in the book, I looked up fencing clubs near me, for the footwork, and boxing at St. Saviour's Amateur Boxing Club in town as well."

The boxing was especially helpful for Hanley's overall improvement as a fighter. "They taught me a lot. You know, Western boxing. Full contact sparring as opposed to the 'flicky' point scoring in competition karate. By 16 or 17, I was pretty proficient in boxing."

Joe Hanley trained in boxing for a year at the St. Saviour's club while maintaining his Kenpo training. Eventually, he had the opportunity to meet someone who knew Bruce Lee personally: the grandmaster of the American Kenpo system, Ed Parker.

Joe Hanley was excited to meet a friend and colleague of Bruce Lee, Ed Parker. (Photo courtesy of Joe Hanley)

"We were in the IKKA – the International Kenpo Karate Association," said Hanley. "We did American Kenpo founded by Ed Parker, and he came over in the early eighties. That was a big deal for everyone in the club, the seniors over me, and the instructor himself. *The founder of the art was coming over*. He came to our club and did weekend workshops. He also appeared on Irish television and did a demonstration."

Hanley finally had an opportunity to talk about Bruce Lee with someone who knew him. "I got to meet Ed Parker and train with him. When he talked about Bruce Lee, I mean, I had the books and had seen pictures of them together. This was a guy who *actually* met Bruce Lee; not only did Ed Parker meet him, he also *trained* with him. I was quite excited, you know? Parker gave me some good advice and told me I was good and that I was very fast, and all of that. I was just on cloud nine meeting Ed Parker."

Despite the progress that Joe Hanley made in martial arts and his continued ambitions, fate would play a hand in bringing that chapter of his life to a close. As it turned out, at the age of 18 and in the best shape of his young life, his heart was a ticking time bomb waiting to explode.

"I'd won the European championship in Dusseldorf and that qualified me to go to the Long Beach tournament which, of course, as you know, Bruce Lee folklore, that's just the Mecca of tournaments," he said. "I would represent Ireland in the 'individuals' categrory, so I was kind of geared up for that. I was training non-stop, and I was fit as a fiddle. Very strong for my age.

"It was January of 1985, and I was just walking through town with a karate teammate of mine, in the City Centre of Dublin. Students were doing blood pressure checks for charitable donations, so I threw my few cents in, and they took my blood pressure. And I was so cocky, I was so sure of my fitness, that I told my teammate, *'Wait until you see this.'* I thought they were gonna just say you're super fit. You know, *'You're like Bruce Lee.'* And the guy doing the blood pressure check says, *'There is something wrong here. Can you hold on there a second?'* And he just ran off."

The student hunted down a supervisor and returned with him to double-check Hanley's blood pressure readings. "He told the supervisor, *'I'm getting this crazy reading off this guy. Is it right? I must not be doing it right. His blood pressure is just through the roof.'* So, the senior guy, the doctor, he took it, and his faced just dropped. He said, *'That's unreal, that blood pressure.'* He said, *'You need to go to a doctor; go now, don't waste time, and go straightaway.'"*

Joe Hanley was disturbed by the experience but did not immediately go to see a doctor. "I kind of dismissed it," he said. "But I did go to the doctor, I think the next day or two. And he said, *'Give me your mother's phone number. You're going straight the hospital.'* So, within a few hours, I was in the Mater Hospital just near me, and they did a battery of tests. I knew there was something wrong. I kept saying to them, *'But I'm fit! I'm fit!'* They were checking, but they couldn't get a pulse in my legs. I saw a team of six or seven doctors around me going, *'I think I hear something. I think I can...what the hell's going on here?'* So anyway, they did a battery of tests over the next day or two. They did an angiogram, and they discovered a deformity in my heart called coarctation of the aorta. That the blood wasn't going through, a blockage. It was twisted. They said, *'We got it; we can see what it is.'* And I told them, *'I don't drink, I don't smoke, I don't even eat sausages. I'm quite fit.'* I told them about my training. And they said no, there was quite an investigation into how I got away with this so long. I was just born with it; it was a congenital heart deformity."

The doctor informed Hanley that his heart could have exploded at any moment, and that his strenuous training was taxing his heart all the more. "The doctor told me that, within six months, I would have just dropped dead. He said I would have been training and my heart would just *pop*. It was under so much pressure to get past this blockage. It was working crazy."

The doctors performed an emergency operation to save Joe Hanley's life. In a six-hour surgery, the medical team pulled Hanley's heart from his body and removed the twisted portion of his aorta, replacing it with a medical device – a synthetic artery that, fortunately, has performed well for Joe Hanley over the last four decades.

It was a long road to recovery for Hanley. He spent four months in the hospital before being released. He was on anti-rejection drugs for months after that while continuing to heal from the surgery to his heart as well as the ribs that were cut to open his chest. A surgical scar stretching halfway across his torso was a permanent reminder of what Hanley had survived. "I told the girls that I survived a shark attack," he joked.

While in his hospital bed recovering, Joe Hanley passed his time drawing. Much of the subject of his drawing was Bruce Lee. "As I was on my hospital bed, I kept drawing, because I draw a lot. I drew Bruce Lee and, you know, he did keep me going through that time, because he meant that much to me. All I thought about was him. And just thinking about Bruce's back injury (what I knew at the time anyway) and how he persevered through it, it made me want to get through what I was going through. I was so strong and fit and everything. I just wanted to get back to training."

Hanley eventually returned to his Kenpo train-

Drawing of Bruce Lee that Joe Hanley drew while he was recovering from heart surgery. (Image courtesy of Joe Hanley)

ing, but things did not exactly return to normal. "I came back and went back to training. A lot of the guys that I used to fight were afraid to hit me because they thought that they might be responsible for re-injuring me. This one guy, in particular, said, *'I can't!'* And I was like, *'Come on!'* But I did try, and, obviously, I protected a bit more than I used protect. But I'd always led with my strongest side in front, like Bruce Lee. So, it was kind of guarded anyway. But they were afraid to do a side kick or something to my ribs, they told me, or a roundhouse; they thought they'd break it. They all came down to see me when I was in hospital, my instructor and the whole senior team of black belts, and so they knew how serious things had been."

A drawing of American Kenpo founder Ed Parker by Joe Hanley. (Image courtesy of Joe Hanley)

Frustrated, Joe Hanley began to drift away from his Kenpo school. He tried to continue training for a year or two longer, but Hanley struggled to regain the physical conditioning that he once possessed. Despite his strong desire to continue, the martial arts period of his life was drawing to a close.

While one door was closing, another was opening. Throughout his teenage years, Hanley continued to draw, refining his artistic talent. "I remember one of the black belts saying to me, when I showed him some of my drawings in the karate club, *'Oh, you're a jack of all trades! You can do anything!'* I said, *'Yeah, but I'm a master of myself.'"*

Focusing on his artistic talent, Hanley secured a job as head of animation with Emerald City Productions, an American-owned animation production company based in Dublin. Emerald City Productions produced animated television films primarily based on literary classics.

The location of the production studio in the Dún Laoghaire area required Hanley to move, drawing him further away from his old haunts. "I moved out of Cabra where I was from and where the Kenpo school was based," he said. "I moved over to the southside of Dublin because I got a job there as a cartoonist and animator. I moved in with a girl over there who was one of the other animators."

Joe Hanley at Emerald City Productions. (Photo courtesy of the Dún Laoghaire-Rathdown County Library)

For a while, Hanley tried to maintain some level of involvement with martial arts. "I still used to travel over, but now I'm 19. And maybe I was growing out of it, you know? Or maybe, and I think sometimes, I have to admit, I felt I'm never going to be as good as I thought I was or was going to be. It sounds silly now. But I said, *I'm not physically perfect anymore, and I've been ripped apart.* And I didn't think I was as fast as I once was. Maybe I just grew out of it. You know, as I said, I started a new job. I moved out of my home; I got a flat over there. I did take up fencing in Sandymount for a bit, which I loved. But that was it. I think I just moved away from it then, but I still had the interest in Bruce Lee.

Joe Hanley continued collecting books and magazines on Bruce Lee. Like many fans of Lee, he found that there were always more layers of the onion to peel back. "I think there was obviously a bit of nostalgia, and I felt he was *mine,*" Hanley said. "Kind of weird. You know, when I heard people talk about him, just even socially, when I was out and something came up about him, I kind of nodded knowingly, because I knew everything about him. I've read every book that was available. I still have all those magazines that people are now collecting from back in the day, I mean, tons and piles. Back then, I would go to the cinema, literally on the big screen, and watch them all the time. And then came the videotapes. That was heaven, as I could watch them at home. It was crazy. I still have the old VHS tapes. So, I kind of felt that he was mine. I see these collectors over in the United States, and my hat's off to those guys. The collect everything. I didn't get to that level. But I think, in Ireland, my collection was probably the biggest."

Joe Hanley worked as an animator for three years. During his time at Emerald City Productions, Hanley animated the films *Ghost Stories* (1987), *The Phantom of the Opera* (1988), and *Les Misérables* (1990). "I was mad into the animation, too," said Hanley. "I just became obsessed with that; I loved it. It was very basic television animation, but it was all new to me, and I'd stay behind late just trying to get this scene right, you know, in the animation." Then an evening out with coworkers changed the course of his life once again.

"I went to see a play, as simple as that," said Hanley. "I'd never been to theater growing up, funnily enough, in Dublin. And while I was animating with the company, one the girls came around – one of the animators – and asked me to go to the theater with a group of friends, the way some people have these nights out, a *'let's all go bowling'* type of thing. Nicola comes in and says, *'We're all going to the theater tonight. It's supposed to be very good. Do you wanna?'* I said, *'Okay, yeah.'* I put my seven or eight bucks in, too, and I went along. It was a Seán O'Casey play at the Gate Theatre, *Juno and the Paycock*. That was '86; it was around that time and I just– it was almost like the *Bruce Lee* thing; I was *nailed* to the back of my seat. Literally, I couldn't

The 1986 run of Juno and the Paycock *at the Gate Theatre in Dublin catalyzed Hanley's interest in acting.* (National Library of Ireland)

Jade Yourell and Joe Hanley in a 1999 production The Importance of Being Earnest by Oscar Wilde (Photo by Aenghus McMahon)

believe it. And it was about Dublin – *working class Dubliners* – my kind of people. I later ended up doing that same play up there; I performed it. And O'Casey's daughter, Shivaun, told me he would have loved to have seen me in it. Yeah, I just went to see theater and I said, *'My God, that was amazing!'* Live! In front of me! With one of our greatest actors, Donal McCann! It just blew me away.

"I started going to the theater every week. Then, at the age of 21, I decided I wanted to try the acting. There weren't many acting schools in Dublin. But the Dublin Youth Theatre was taking students from age 16 to 22. It was free, near me, and they did plays. I didn't know any actors, I went along to a kind of workshop audition, and I hadn't a clue. But I got in. And it was not a drama school, it was more like a youth club; instead of ping pong or games, they did plays. They did one or two big productions a year that were reviewed in the *Irish Times*, along with professional shows, and they'd do a lot of series of one-act plays.

"I did that for a year and a half while I was still working in animation, and then a professional director came to see one of the shows we were in, and she was looking for actors for smaller parts in her production. It had a few lines in it; it was a Caryl Churchill play, and she picked two of us from the group. She came to see us doing workshops and casting in it. Suddenly I'm in the theater

Enda Oates, Joe Hanley, Liana O'Cleirigh, and Mick Nolan in Fair City. (Beta Bajgart/RTÉArchives)

in town performing. I get paid for it. Now, it wasn't much; I think it was 50 bucks a week or something, whatever it was, but I was an ensemble player. But that was it, and I knew by then I was off anyway, that this was what I wanted to do. So I wrote my resignation to the American boss, and he wasn't happy. Nor was my mother, my poor mother. She was telling me, *'What the hell are you doing? You fecking eejit! You want to be an actor?'* I said, *'I do, I do. I think I can do it.'* She couldn't believe it."

Hanley did theater work for a few years and managed to find consistent work. Then a producer from Radio Telefís Éireann (RTÉ), Ireland's public broadcaster, came to see him. The producer bore an offer.

"That new soap that recently started, *Fair City*, there is a part in that for you," said the producer. "Would you be interested in doing a couple of weeks?"

"I said, *'Yeah, sure.'* I hadn't even seen it," said Hanley. "It had only been on for six months or seven months. That's how I joined *Fair City*. It was only a cameo sort of thing, just popping in every few weeks or once a month, and I was still doing theater as well. But then, eventually, after the next season, they offered me a full contract, and I became a regular part of the cast."

Joe Hanley played the popular character Hughie Phelan on the Irish soap opera for several years. During that time, he also began appearing in movies, including *The Run of the Country* (1995) and *Michael Collins* (1996).

Hanley's popularity on *Fair City* led to some interesting situations for the actor. During a break from filming of *Fair City*, Joe Hanley filmed his small role in *Michael Collins*. While filming, Hanley went drinking with castmates Liam Neeson, Alan Rickman, Brendan Gleeson, and Aidan Quinn.

As Hanley tells the story: "Liam actually said, *'Will you go for a drink lads?'* Just a nearby hotel in Temple Bar.' We agreed.

"We found this quiet hotel nearby, and I was having a pint with Liam, Alan, Brendan, and Aidan. As we were drinking in a quiet corner, the door opens and these young women come in all dolled up for a hen night. They looked over our way and became excited. *'Ah, would you look who it is! Valerie! Camilla!* They all ran over to us, and they went, *'It's Hughie out of Fair City!'* And they had napkins and beer mats and they were saying, *'Could you sign this?'*

Joe Hanley in *Michael Collins (1996)*. (Warner Brothers)

"So, I was signing these autographs and Alan Rickman was looking at me and Liam Neeson was saying, *'What's going on here?'* The women were oblivious to all of them. And I'm going, *'Yes. Who is it to?'* And off they went. Liam said, *'What was all that about?'* And I said, *'Ah, it's just a bit of television I do.'"*

While *Fair City* brought Joe Hanley a measure of fame, it became a poisoned chalice for the actor. While it was good, steady work, the schedule didn't allow him to do much theater. Missing the professional and artistic opportunities that theater work afforded him, Hanley announced his exit from *Fair City* in 1997.

After leaving *Fair City,* Hanley dived back into theater work, appearing in two-to-three plays a year, including engagements in London's West End, Edinburgh, Heidelberg, and throughout Ireland. He appeared in a number of film productions, including *Agnes Browne* (2000), *The Count of Monte Cristo* (2002), *Veronica Guerin*

(2003), and *Batman Begins* (2005). He also guest-starred in multiple television shows, among them *The Clinic* (2007), *Murphy's Law* (2007), and the television mini-series *Empire* (2005).

Over the years, the producers of *Fair City* approached Joe Hanley about returning to the television show, and when actress Joan O'Hara (who played the mother of his character Hughie Phelan) passed away in 2007, Hanley agreed to return to *Fair City* so that his character could attend his mother's funeral. A second appearance in 2014 to attend the funeral of Hughie Phelan's brother led to a permanent return to the show in 2015.

"I did enjoy being back after being out for more or less 17 years," said Hanley. "The theater was going well. It was a grand life, but it was a lot of traveling, and I was getting older. I actually enjoyed the feeling of being back in front of the camera. So, I said yeah. I came back for a month or two, then they said we should do another three months. I did that. And I've been back as a regular for over nine years now."

Phelin Drew, Joe Hanley, and Keith Hanna are seen as The Abbey Theatre hosts photocall ahead of the opening of The Risen People by James Plunkett. (Alamy)

Joe Hanley has a number of accomplishments on his résumé. Champion martial artist, visual artist and animator, and professional actor. However, one creative endeavor that he has yet to undertake, but would like to accomplish, is writing a play. Hanley has a deeply personal idea for the play, one that would draw from his own life and struggles, and, specifically, touch on his special relationship with Bruce Lee.

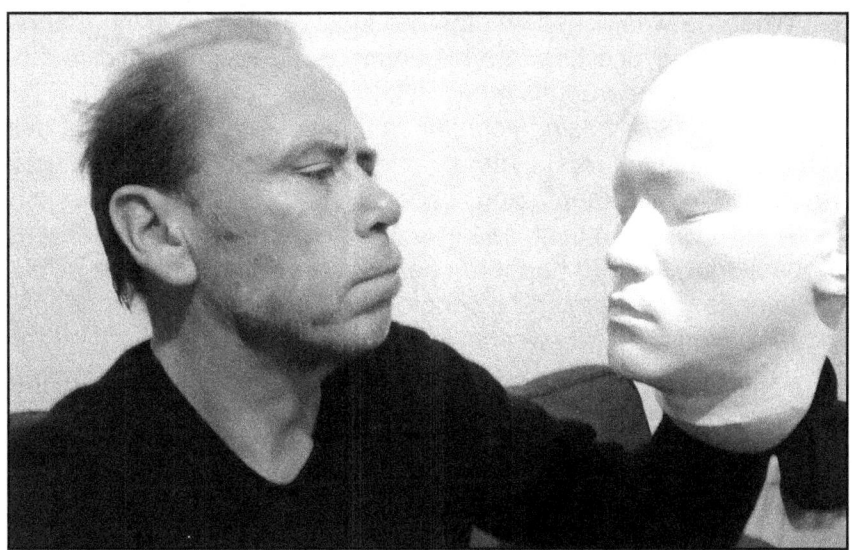

Alas, poor Bruce. I knew him. (Photo courtesy of Joe Hanley)

"I've often thought about it, and then I tell myself no," he said. "I tried writing down some thoughts, but I'm not a writer, and I try scribbling down a few little things, you know, and I always get lost. Maybe I'll get someone to help me. I've told a few writers about it, and they wanted to make it into a play, but it is important that it is my story. And Bruce Lee is at the heart of it. It should be as I'm telling you now, about how Bruce affected me and my upbringing. Because I didn't have my father, you know, I didn't know who my father was. I never had an idea. I didn't find out until I was nearly 30. And looking back, was that why I became so obsessed with Bruce Lee? This father figure, this superhero guy who represented something I didn't have growing up. Yeah, Bruce Lee as a father figure."

Hopefully, in the near future, Joe Hanley's story about his remarkable life and how Bruce Lee inspired him will be told on a theater stage. For now, he continues with his role on RTÉ's *Fair City*, his beloved stage work (most recently in a well-received run of performances as "Bill" in Martin McDonagh's *Hangmen* at the Gaiety Theatre), and the occasional guest appearance in television and film. A recent offer to lecture on acting at Dublin's historic Trinity College is even under consideration.

Now in his late 50s, Hanley continues to be inspired and fascinated by Bruce Lee. "He was a really big hero to me – still is, I think. I still get a kick out of looking at photos that I haven't seen. *Wow, I didn't see that one!* I still look up to him."

When he was asked whether he incorporates anything that he learned from Bruce Lee into his acting, Hanley thought for a moment and then offered his reply.

"*Honestly expressing yourself.* You know, I try to keep that one in mind. I just think what a remarkable human being Bruce Lee was, you know, just to keep going, because he says it in that interview with Pierre Berton. I think he knew then that the *Warrior* series was probably not going to happen. I believe he was notified of it before the interview, perhaps the day before. But then he said, '*It doesn't matter as long as you honestly express yourself.*' It doesn't matter. It'll happen. Like Bruce Lee, I've been honestly expressing myself for some time now."

After answering the question, Joe Hanley had another thought. "Also, *simplicity*. To keep it simple. Like it said in the *Tao of Jeet Kune Do,* it is very hard, indeed, to convey simplicity. Something like that. It's very difficult indeed. So, I do try to keep it simple."

In 2018, Joe Hanley fulfilled a life-long dream and visited the gravesites of Bruce and Brandon Lee in Seattle. (Photo courtesy of Joe Hanley)

Perhaps the greatest and most privileged fan of Bruce Lee has been writer *John Little*. A fan of Lee since childhood, Little was given the enviable task of editing Bruce Lee's previously unpublished notes, writings, letters, and interviews into the seven-volume *Bruce Lee Library Series,* as well as writing or editing seven more books on the subject of the martial arts legend. In addition to that, Little directed three films on Lee: *Bruce Lee: In His Own Words* (1998), *Bruce Lee: A Warrior's Journey* (2000), and *Bruce Lee: In Pursuit of the Dragon* (2009). He served as director of the Bruce Lee Educational Foundation in the late 1990s and early 2000s.

Author and filmmaker John Little. (Author's archives)

"I have been an ardent, zealous fan of Bruce Lee since I was 12," said Little. "I used to read everything about him I could get my hands on. I remember I'd go down to Chinatown in Toronto and pick up all the Chinese language magazines that would come across to Canada in the mid-to-late 1970s. Then I would take them back home and get Chinese friends to translate them and look at the pictures. I even snuck into a screening of his films with a hand-held 8mm camera and filmed them. Then I would go back and watch them on a viewer. It was great because watching Bruce and the way he moved his body and the way he executed his techniques allowed me to practice that through the aid of that viewer and a mirror. When we actually had a karate school that opened down the street from me a year or so later, I was able to advance to green belt within about a week because of the dexterity I had gotten from imitating Bruce.

"I was fascinated with Bruce Lee, always was, but as you grow older you begin to think that it's time to put away childish things and become a man. You get married. You have responsibility. You attempt to justify what could be viewed as adolescent hero worship. But it always struck me that Bruce Lee had more to offer.

"Bruce wasn't just a guy who could throw a baseball with great velocity, a person who was a one-time heavyweight champion, or, in my case living in Canada, a guy who could put the puck in the net. He had a philosophy, and it was the philosophy I found myself getting more and more fascinated by. And as for his physical fitness, he was a man who was just in awesome physical fitness! His physique was tremendous!"

Little said that Bruce Lee is an unparalleled role model. "To me, when I was growing up, Bruce represented the perfect male: he was tremendously well built and a good-looking guy. He was intelligent, and he had a philosophy. He was successful. He was married and had children. He was doing work that he loved. He had a creative vein, and I decided that was it! That's what everybody should aspire to! But none of the books that came out had any information on how he trained or how he built his body. That led to my own (sort of using Bruce's philosophical principles) researching the science or the facts of Bruce's physical fitness and muscle physiology. Long story short, that in turn took me to California where I got to meet Brandon Lee."

Little was writing for Joe Weider's bodybuilding magazine *Muscle and Fitness* when he was assigned to write an article on Bruce Lee's weight training methods. As part of the interview, Little had the opportunity to interview Brandon Lee, Bruce Lee's son.

"It was like he ripped a veil off of past memories and brought it all back," said Little. "I realized that Bruce and Brandon's philosophy dealt with what Brandon called *'real world applications'*. It had to be truthful; it had to be real. It couldn't be artificial or pragmatic. So it was hard for me to leave that mindset and go back to interview a champion bodybuilder who was going to tell me why it was life and death to have 20-inch arms, you know. I couldn't square it anymore. It just didn't make sense.

"Anyway, I was with *Muscle and Fitness* magazine when I did the article on Bruce. The nice thing about working for Joe Weider at the time was that it gave me the opportunity to speak to people and pursue areas of fitness that previously might not have been open to me. And certainly, the first opportunity I had to flex my muscle in that domain was to do something on Bruce Lee and that was his training methods. That's how I met Linda."

That first meeting with Linda Lee Cadwell would eventually result in the *Bruce Lee Library Series* project. "The *Bruce Lee Library Series* came about as the result of a friendship I developed with

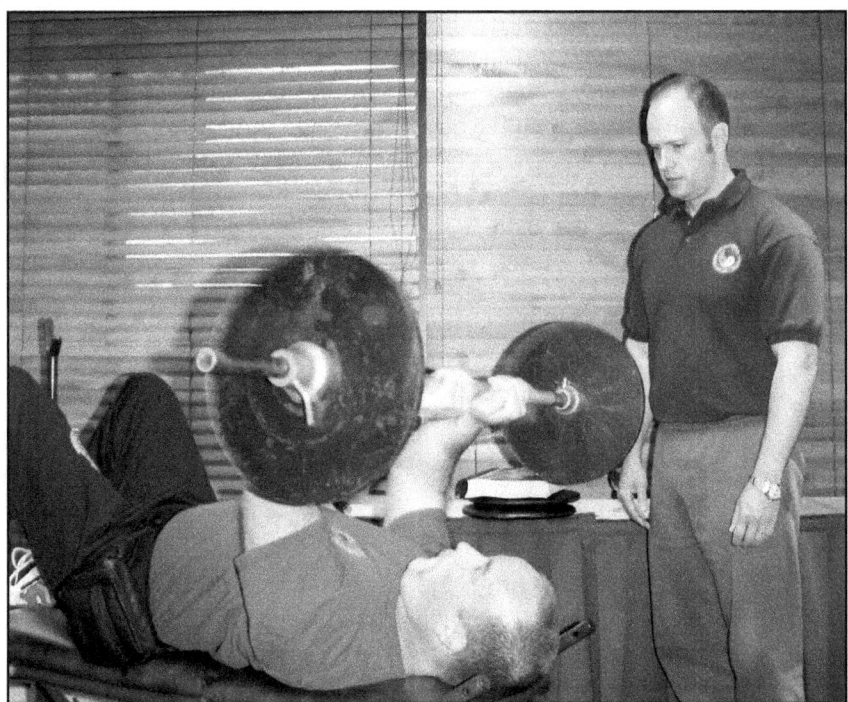

John Little's experience as a bodybuilder and writer was his entry point into the world of Bruce Lee. Here Little explains Lee's weight-training methodology. (Author's archives)

Linda Lee Cadwell, who is Bruce's widow," said John Little. "She invited me up to Idaho to look through Bruce's papers, initially with the idea of doing a book on his training methods, which has since become *The Art of Expressing the Human Body*. But while I was there, I was just stunned at the wealth of material, particularly the non-martial art material. It just opened up a whole new vista of perspective on Bruce Lee for me because, like most people, I knew he was intelligent and I knew he had a philosophy, but, from my perspective, it was a philosophy that dealt solely with the martial arts. Well, *how wrong I was!* He was a philosopher first and the martial arts were but one expression of it. His filmmaking was another expression of it. His interactions with people and friends and his business dealings were others, as was his training and physical fitness methods. I was just delighted, I was like a kid in Aladdin's cave, being able to see papers that nobody but Bruce Lee had seen – in some instances, since he wrote them – such as annotations in the margins of his books and little philosophical jottings that he had done enclosed within the pages of a book. There was everything:

correspondence, daytimer diaries, the whole bit. It was like going to Bruce Lee University and learning all these different courses that were the *totality* of the man. And it was something that was great because I learned something new about him every day.

"I was surprised by so much of it, because it was new and personal," said Little about the writings. "I guess the most striking thing about it was how prolific a writer he was. Again, here's a man who passed away at the age of 32 and did the bulk of his writings during an eight-year period. And yet, my first time returning to California from Boise, from visiting with Linda, I returned with 60 pounds of photocopied material! I had to make a subsequent trip, and I came back with about 30 pounds worth!"

John Little in the Bruce Lee Estate archives.

Little laughed. "*This is not an ordinary martial artist.* To have over 2,500 books as he does in his library, the bulk of which are philosophy books, just shows that his martial art wasn't created in a vacuum. It was created out of much thought, and that's philosophic method. That's mind training. His mind was certainly the organ Bruce Lee trained every day. That's what gave birth to his art."

Studying the archives of Bruce Lee gave John Little a new perspective on Lee; it also made him realize that many of the things commonly believed about Bruce Lee were the result of misunderstandings. One area in which John Little believes people commonly misunderstand Lee regards his art of Jeet Kune Do. "There's a popular misconception that he took the 'best' of a bunch of different arts and created his own art. For one thing, he would be vehemently opposed to any notion of the 'best', because there is no 'best'. What's best in one second might be the worst in the next. The whole idea that he combined a bunch of styles and that's what Jeet Kune Do is, the idea of styles itself, was repugnant to Bruce Lee. Think of it: a synonym for 'style' to Bruce Lee would have been a cage. So, the idea is not to combine a bunch of cages, the idea is to be free of cages or to be free of 'styles' and find out what it means to function in the totality of your humanity. It's simply a way of finding out what is an efficient way for a human being to move in combat and not be hung up or confined to any sort of blanket approach to how you are going to act in a combat situation. So, there are those misperceptions that have been popularized."

In the beginning, jumping ship from a steady job writing for *Muscle and Fitness* to the uncertainty of being a self-employed author came with challenges. There were times while compiling the first Bruce Lee books that Little and his family struggled financially. John Little recalled, at one point, searching for a place to sell the family's only vehicle in order to pay bills. On another occasion, he remembered Ted Wong buying groceries so that Little's family could eat. Yet, Little knew that the work he was doing was important and would eventually pay off.

Ted Wong was particularly kind to John Little. In 1995, Little learned that Bruce Lee's personal weightlifting machine, a Marcy circuit trainer, was in the possession of LaSalle College in Kowloon, where Linda Lee donated it after the death of her husband. To John Little, being a bodybuilder and fitness expert, the machine was the holy grail of Bruce Lee memorabilia. LaSalle was willing to give Little the machine, but he would have to pay to have it shipped to the United States. Unable to afford the cost of shipping, Ted Wong generously stepped in and paid for shipping the device to Little's home.

One of John Little's most important contriibutions to Bruce Lee fandom was the release of the Pierre Berton interview. (Author's archive)

One of the most important accomplishments of John Little during the 1990s was the acquisition of Canadian broadcaster Pierre Berton's interview with Bruce Lee – the only English-language television interview of Lee known to exist. Long sought by collectors and fans of Bruce Lee, the best a fan could hope for at the time was to get a poor-quality snippet of the interview circulating on VHS tape. But Little, having grown up watching the Pierre

Berton show in his native Canada, decided to ask Berton himself if the complete interview was available to view. To his surprise, Berton not only said the master tape still existed, he also offered Little the rights to it. Along with an investment partner, John Little bought the rights and released a complete and pristine edition of it on home media as *Bruce Lee: The Lost Interview,* making the interview available to fans for the first time since its initial broadcast.

Little is proud that he was able to give that important recording to the fans. "I think that is a historical document, and I'm glad that I had a hand in unearthing it," he said.

John Little understands the inspirational effect that Bruce Lee has on people in all walks of life. "It's funny, with Bruce you read about his life story, his views, and how he dealt with adversity, and you realize that anything is possible. I would have never, in a million years, guessed that I would be doing something that I love, which is telling people about the significance of Bruce Lee. I never would have guessed that that would have been a possibility."

John Little took great pride in producing the short film, *Bruce Lee: In His Own Words*. "I was able to do a film in which Bruce was given a platform to speak for himself about his life, his art, and his career. What I like, and what I think is why I feel so strongly about it, is that it is so important to let him speak for himself, not to get it second-hand or to rely on someone's faded memory of what he said or how he believed because, by and large, everyone who has claimed to be his representative has been wrong. His words reveal that."

Other fans agree. "That's why I appreciate John Little," said Robert Blakeman. "He's helping to clear up the confusion."

Bruce Lee: In His Own Words came about as the result of John Little's involvement in Warner Brothers' 1998 home video release of *Enter the Dragon*. "I was asked by Warner Brothers to create a short documentary as a special feature for the 1998 release," said Little. The film he produced excited the executives at Warner Brothers. "Warner Brothers stuck a 16mm print of it to be shown in a limited theatrical release," said Little, "in order for it to be considered for an Academy Award."

While the film did not win an Oscar, it did take home top prizes at the Toronto International Film Festival and the Montreal World Film Festival. "It was pretty heady," recalled Little, "as was beating out Marty Scorsese's short film at the Toronto International Short Film Festival for Best Documentary, particularly with Linda Lee Cadwell seated next to me for the screening."

John Little's short film, Bruce Lee: In His Own Words. *won first prize for documentary at the Toronto International Film Festival and first prize for short film at the Montreal World Film Festival.* (Los Angeles Times)

John Little followed that documentary up with another, perhaps even more ambitious, film. Off the success of Little's *Bruce Lee: In His Own Words*, Warner Brothers greenlit *Bruce Lee: A Warrior's Journey* with a modest budget of $130,000. The project began as a dream on Little's part to realize Bruce Lee's vision for his unfinished film *Game of Death*. The idea came to Little years earlier when he discovered Lee's script and directorial notes for the unfinished film. As luck would have it, lost footage from the filming of *Game of Death* was recently discovered by Bey Logan in the archives of Golden Harvest and made available to Little for his project. All the stars seemed to be in alignment.

Bruce Lee: A Warrior's Journey was a documentary on the making of *Game of Death* that concluded with a presentation of the footage shot by Bruce Lee and reconstructed in the manner Lee en-

John Little, on the set of Bruce Lee: A Warrior's Journey, *directing a scene.* (Photo courtesy of John Little)

visioned. Part of the documentary was filmed on location in South Korea, where Bruce Lee intended to shoot exteriors. The film was a labor of love for John Little, so much so that when Bruce Lee's co-star Kareem Abdul-Jabbar demanded a payment of $30,000 to sit for an interview for the documentary, a figure that was not in the production budget, Little gave up his payment for the production to ensure Abdul-Jabbar's participation. To help pay for post-production, Little also wrote a companion book for the documentary.

"Assembling the *Game of Death* footage according to Bruce's surviving script notes, flying to South Korea and filming the storyline, and putting that into a documentary was very fulfilling," said Little. "I kept recalling the first time I saw a photo from that film of Bruce and Kareem Abdul-Jabbar inside Alex Ben Block's book *The Legend of Bruce Lee,* which I read in 1974. The caption under the photo said something to the effect that the film was *'never completed or released.'* It was nice to have been able to lend Bruce my hands, so to speak, to complete and release it."

While producing the two documentaries, John Little still maintained his responsibilities as literary executor and official historian for the Bruce Lee Estate, as well as his responsibilities as a member of the Jun Fan Jeet Kune Do Nucleus. Little produced the seventh volume in the *Bruce Lee Library Series,* which, at that point, had sold over 500,000 copies. He continued his efforts to allow Bruce Lee to speak for himself with the book *Bruce Lee: Words from a Master* and authored the book *The Warrior Within,* which explored how Bruce Lee's personal philosophies can enrich the readers' lives. At the same time, Little continued writing and editing *Bruce Lee Magazine* and the Jun Fan Jeet Kune Do Nucleus newsletter.

The cast and crew of Bruce Lee: A Warrior's Journey *on location in South Korea. In the background is the buddha statue that Bruce Lee visualized in his script notes.* (Photo courtesy of John Little)

In Fall of 1998, the Jun Fan Jeet Kune Do Nucleus announced the formation of a new organization, the Bruce Lee Educational Foundation. John Little was named as its director. In the announcement of its formation, Little wrote: "A monumental decision regarding the structure and focus of this organization was reached at the last meeting of your Board of Directors (The Nucleus). Our main goal has always been *'to educate interested persons about the life, art and philosophy of Bruce Lee.'* However, it has evolved that the main interest of those 'interested persons' has been in the area of the physical martial art that Bruce taught and practiced in his lifetime. Therefore, in order to bring greater focus to the educational priorities that form our true mission, it was decided to establish an umbrella or parent organization called the Bruce Lee Educational Foundation. There will be several branches under its auspices, one of which is *Jun Fan Jeet Kune Do,* which concerns itself mainly with the physical martial art. The other branches would be 1) the *Philos-*

The rebranding as the Bruce Lee Educational Foundation was intended to broaden the focus of the organization beyond the martial arts. Little is seen here at the first conference after he was appointed director. (Author's archives)

ophy/Education branch, to be an based on the Krishnamurti Foundation template and involved in Bruce's research into the sciences, philosophy, physiology, psychology, filmmaking, motivational studies, and teaching methods, and 2) the *Historical* branch involving the compilation of oral and written history of Bruce and his art, and the creating of a permanent archive to preserve his writings, photos, video and audio tapes, films and memorabilia."

John Little's main personal objective for the Bruce Lee Educational Foundation was to elevate Bruce Lee's philosophical ideas in the public's consciousness. One of his goals was to plan a series of symposiums on the philosophy of Bruce Lee in universities across the United States and the world. "I think if we are to be serious about advancing Bruce Lee's thought, we need to conduct these symposiums and educate people – not about fighting the battle without, but rather fighting the battle within; against the dragons of ignorance, fear, and prejudice."

Little's ideas for the symposiums were dynamic and diverse. "I can see films, videos, slide presentations, audio, dialogues, question-and-answer sections, and readings. And we should obtain a good cross-section of people from different backgrounds and viewpoints, not simply academics or theorists."

Little envisioned the symposiums as being largely divorced from the martial art aspect of Bruce Lee's legacy. "Bruce Lee's legacy as a martial artist is already well-settled; having a group of martial artists relate, by rote, a series of techniques or self-defense maneuvers is not what we are attempting to convey (i.e., the seriousness and relevance of Bruce's thought to social problems). I think it is self-defeating to advance a position of Bruce being *'more than fighting'* and then pause for a quick demonstration on fighting techniques that Bruce Lee favored. I'm open to be challenged on this point, but, for the moment, I think it would be both unnecessary and potentially (to certain groups of people who might benefit from hearing Bruce's thought) alienating."

Given that most were martial artists, it was unsurprising that John Little would face opposition to his efforts from the Nucleus. Not every member of the organization's board of directors was supportive of promoting Bruce Lee as a philosopher; some were outright dismissive of the idea, including a member of Bruce Lee's own family. However, there was no denying that the idea was gaining traction with the release of John Little's books and documentaries.

In June of 2000, Little was busy completing work on *Bruce Lee: A Warrior's Journey*. "*The Warrior's Journey* project has been incredibly demanding," he said at the time, "as it must be if it is to be done properly. I've just finished my rough cut of this film and, by reports from Warner Brothers and Linda Lee Cadwell, they were 'blown away' it, which is wonderful news to me, personally, but also to Bruce's legacy and intention for the film."

Despite the accolades, Little was feeling the strain of his workload and many commitments. "I've had to work simultaneously on the film, on a book on the film, on two issues of the newsletter, and two issues of the magazine. I have just completed all of this and now feel like I have finally been given an opportunity to catch my breath."

The first of what John Little envisioned as a series of symposiums on Bruce Lee's philosophy occurred in the Fall of 2000 with two historic lectures on the philosophy of Bruce Lee at universities in Northern Ireland and the Republic of Ireland. On behalf of the Bruce Lee Educational Foundation, Little, along with Taky Kimura's son, Andy Kimura, and James Bishop, the author of this book, traveled to the Irish isle in September of 2000 to speak on Bruce Lee's philosophy at Queen's University in Belfast and Trinity College in Dublin.

John Little with social worker Jim Deery touring the New Lodge area of Belfast, Northern Ireland. (Author's archives)

"The most important part of the lectures that we gave in Ireland," said Little, "was the opportunity to present Bruce Lee's philosophy for the first time in an academic setting. I had attempted to do that in Boise, Idaho at Boise State University, but I couldn't get an audience; the academic gatekeepers were not interested in letting Bruce Lee in when they could teach subjects on Immanuel Kant, Socrates, or Plato – the big wheels in philosophy. So, to get this opportunity, and in Ireland of all places, was phenomenal, because I'd always wanted to go to Ireland, and this was an opportunity to marry two big interests of mine: to share Bruce's philosophy and visit the land of my ancestors. So that I was able to blend both of those together was tremendous."

The sponsor of the Irish speaking tour was Martin O'Neill, a senior social worker in Northern Ireland. As part of the tour, the Bruce Lee Educational Foundation delegation visited places of social and historical interest, including the New Lodge area of Belfast, where the delegation met social worker Jim Deery and learned about the struggles in Northern Ireland known as the Troubles.

The entire experience was significant for John Little. "The trip made a lasting impact on me," he said. "It was fascinating to see those venerated institutions, which we only read about at that time. To go into Trinity College, for example, and see the Book of Kells was fascinating. Speaking in Trinity College in Dublin and Queen's University in Belfast, traveling the countryside and meeting with the Irish people, was inspiring to me. I would also say that the work that Martin O'Neill and Jim Deery were doing was eye opening. So, the cool thing wasn't just to go in and speak in the abstract about Bruce Lee's philosophy, but to actually see a practical application of it in the field of social work was fascinating."

John Little lecturing at the Bruce Lee philosophy symposium in Belfast, Northern Ireland. (Author's archives)

A few weeks after returning from Ireland, On October 22, 2000, *Bruce Lee: A Warrior's Journey* had its premiere at San Francisco's Chinese Cultural Center. A question-and-answer period took place after the showing of the film; John Little was all smiles as he absorbed the compliments from an appreciative audience. Also in attendance was Linda Lee Cadwell, Bruce Lee's daughter, Shannon Lee, and actor Bob Wall.

Things seemed to be moving along nicely for the wide release of *Bruce Lee: A Warrior's Journey*. Warner Brothers was very optimistic about the retail outlook for the film; it was scheduled to be released on home media in Spring of 2001. However, storms were on the horizon.

On March 31, 2001, John Little appeared at the UK's Bruce and Brandon Lee Association annual conference in Bradford, West Yorkshire. He gave a talk on Bruce Lee's philosophy and hosted a showing of *Bruce Lee: A Warrior's Journey*.

While he was his usual engaging self with the attendees, the

John Little appearing at the Bruce and Brandon Lee Association Conference in March 2001. (Photo courtesy of Carl Fox)

event organizers could tell that something was going on with Little behind the scenes. When not fulfilling his obligations for the conference, Little was sequestered in his hotel room on the phone with parties back in the United States.

One of the conference organizers, Carl Fox, recalled John Little acknowledging that a problem existed during their final dinner together that weekend. "We went for dinner on the Saturday night, and John said he'd been on the phone to his wife, Terri," said Fox. Privately, Little admitted to organizers of the Bradford event that things were complicated between him and the Bruce Lee Estate, now controlled by Shannon Lee.

While things seemed comfortable with John Little and the Lee family just five months earlier in October 2000, by March, John Little found himself under a barrage of legal fire from the new law firm representing the Bruce Lee Estate.

Carl Fox recalls the stress that Little was under. "His wife told him, *'Another letter has come, John.'* He said the letters from Shannon Lee's lawyers were arriving daily."

There was a sense of finality in the air. "He didn't say anything publicly," said Fox, "but we knew it was probably the last time he'd make the visit in that capacity."

Little believed that his legal problems with the estate began when he declined a request by the estate to sign over the rights to the Pierre Berton/Bruce Lee interview. The problems began when John Little received a valuation of the rights to the interview. He was told that he could possibly get up to a million dollars for the rights. Little informed Linda Lee Cadwell of what he was told. Cadwell, who had recently turned over management of the Bruce Lee Estate to her daughter, Shannon Lee, suggested that he contact her daughter if he was thinking to sell the rights.

John Little did as Bruce Lee's widow suggested and a meeting with the Bruce Lee Estate's new lawyers was arranged. However, when he met with the lawyers, they expected Little to simply *give* the estate the rights, even though Little purchased the rights directly from Pierre Berton's production company and had a considerable investment in it – not to mention an investment partner, Bob Wolff, who also had a stake in the rights.

"It was the lawyers, with Shannon listening in on speakerphone, who suggested I should simply give it to her," said Little, "more or less as a token of my gratitude toward them for choosing me to write the books." He declined their suggestion.

The lawyers, on behalf of Shannon Lee and the Bruce Lee Estate, responded by taking exception to the things John Little produced during his time as the estate's historian. They registered a legal objection to Tuttle Publishing regarding the agreement to publish the Bruce Lee Library Series; as a result, Little's royalties on the books were frozen.

The lawyers also objected to the release of *Bruce Lee: A Warrior's Journey,* dragging Warner Brothers into the conflict. Their reasons for objecting to the release were unclear. "It was just a generic disapproval," said Little, "using the word *'content'* to be deliberately vague." The last-minute legal complaint from the Bruce Lee Estate's lawyers delayed Warner Brothers' plans for the release of the film.

The conflict over *Bruce Lee: A Warrior's Journey* was especially confusing to John Little, given that Linda Lee Cadwell saw a rough cut in June, and both Cadwell and Shannon Lee sat through the final cut with him at the premiere in October. Cadwell even promoted the film and Little's work in media appearances alongside him.

"She was fine with it right up until the new lawyers came in," said Little about Cadwell. "She even sent me a very complementary fax about the film."

Chris Kent, a member of the Jun Fan Jeet Kune Do Nucleus and a friend of Little, could see the effect the legal troubles were having on him. "What I saw was John's devastation at the walls just closing down around him."

John Little, for his part, had enough of the drama. After returning home from Bradford, Little wrote a letter to the Bruce Lee Educational Foundation board of directors announcing his resignation. Severing his ties with both the foundation and the Lee Estate, Little exited the Bruce Lee business.

Little asked his friend Chris Kent to read his resignation letter to the Nucleus members at their next board meeting, which was held during the annual conference in Holland. He also gave Kent a videotape copy of the new and unreleased *Bruce Lee: A Warrior's Journey* documentary. "He gave me a copy of the finished product to take to Holland," said Kent. "And he said, *'I'm going to leave the decision to you as to whether you want them to see the film or not. And then I'd like you to also read this letter.'* So, I made the decision to allow them to see it."

In Holland, after showing the completed documentary to the Nucleus members, Kent read the letter of resignation from John Little. "His letter was, you know, as usual with John, very positive and praising everything about his time with the organization and the people he met. It was his usual fashion. He kept it on a high level."

However, Chris Kent wasn't done addressing the Nucleus. "After I finished reading John's letter, I said, *'Now I have to read you another letter,'* which was my own letter of resignation. You know, which I kept positive as well."

While the Nucleus was surprised and upset to see Chris Kent resign, there was little concern for John Little's departure; some Nucleus members even celebrated it. The simmering resentment toward Little's popularity and his emphasis on Bruce Lee's philosophy started bubbling to the surface; several Nucleus members expressed happiness at the turn of the events, saying that the focus would finally be moved away from the "psychobabble".

"NEWSWORTHY NOTES"

JOHN LITTLE RESIGNS:
We were saddened to learn of John Little's decision to resign from the Bruce Lee Educational Foundation. He sent a letter of resignation to our seminar in The Netherlands for our board members to read. He expressed that he looked upon the nucleus members as extended family and commended our organization for its work. We accepted his resignation and wish him well in his future endeavors.

CHRIS KENT RESIGNS:
Along with John, Chris Kent also tendered his resignation at the seminar in Holland. Chris, who attended and taught at the seminar, expressed a desire to focus his energies elsewhere. Chris has been with us since inception and his contributions have been many. The board tried to persuade him to change his mind and reinvest his passion, but alas, we accept his resignation and wish him well.

A tale of two notices. From the *Knowing is Not Enough* newsletter, vol. 4, No. 4.

While the Nucleus, as a group, was not grieving the loss of Little, the attendees of the annual conference were a different matter. "I was at the Holland Nucleus seminar with two of my students," said Martin O'Neill. "We were shocked that John Little had resigned his position, as he was a champion of Bruce Lee's martial art and philosophy. I considered him a good friend. He was a great supporter of my community relations work in Northern Ireland and immediately made the connection with Bruce's stance on fighting oppression and racism. We may not see Bruce's other writings published, as John's work has not been followed up by the estate or the foundation."

O'Neill's concerns were warranted and, ultimately, proven true. The Bruce Lee Library series was only seven books into a planned twelve-volume series. Two other books were already finished and were in the possession of publisher Tuttle. The next book in the series was compiled as an "autobiography" of Bruce Lee. It contained all the commentary Lee wrote about his own life, his statements in interviews, and his "daytimers", a sort of diary/planner that he kept for a few years. The book that followed was to be focused on Bruce Lee's artwork, showing his drawing and sketches, many of which have never been seen before. A third book, focused on Lee's movie *Way of the Dragon,* would have contained Bruce Lee's script and production notes, among other things, but Little had not begun the book at the time he exited the Bruce Lee world. Little notified Tuttle that he was canceling the publication of further books, and the existing manuscripts were destroyed.

John Little and his wife decided their next course of action was to take their family back to their native Canada. There was only one problem: with the royalties from the Bruce Lee books frozen, the family was suffering a cashflow problem and did not have the money to make the move. Reluctantly, Little sold Bruce Lee's Marcy circuit trainer (the one Ted Wong paid to have shipped from Hong Kong as a gift to him six years before). He sold it for $40,000 to an heir of the Walmart fortune, the son of Sam Walton's first employee.

Not shackled by the legal complications in the United States, Warner Brothers released *Bruce Lee: A Warrior's Journey* in the UK on home media in October 2001. Fully a year after its premiere in San Francisco, the documentary was still unavailable in the United States.

The film was finally released in the United States on March 26, 2002. There was no fanfare for its release, no marketing campaign by Warner Brothers. The documentary was released in a barebones DVD devoid of the customary extras that would normally be expected of a Bruce Lee film. Warner Brothers quietly, and with the least amount of effort, washed their hands of it.

On July 2, 2002, *Bruce Lee: A Warrior's Journey* made its broadcast debut on the American Movie Classics channel. John Little was asked by the basic cable channel to come into the studio and provide some on-camera commentary for the North American broadcast premiere. He declined the offer.

If the intention of the Bruce Lee Estate's legal team was to finnancially starve John Little into acquiescing to their demands for the rights to the Pierre Berton/Bruce Lee interview, it did not succeed. Little quickly moved on to his next project, serving a similar role as literary executor for the estate of Will Durant, the Pulitzer Prize-winning philosopher and historian. Where once he struggled to convince the world that Bruce Lee was a philosopher, Little now oversaw the literary legacy of a philosophical giant whose 1926 book, *The Story of Philosophy,* launched publisher Simon and Schuster and was credited with introducing philosophy to more Americans than any other book in history.

In his time as literary executor of the Will Durant Estate, Little re-established the Will Durant Foundation and edited and released a number of unpublished books from the historian's archives. He also produced two documentaries on Will Durant and branched out by producing documentaries on philosopher Ayn Rand and Rand's philosophical successor, Leonard Piekoff.

Outside of his philosophical work, Little co-wrote a book on Wing Chun and produced two documentaries around the subject. "The Wing Chun book was done to help out a friend who had some interesting insights into the art that I thought should be published," explained Little. "The documentaries (*Wong Shun Leung: The King of Talking Hands* and the special feature *Wing Chun: The Art That Introduced Kung Fu to Bruce Lee*) were the result of my wanting to learn more about the legendary origins of the art, which resulted in a trip to the Shaolin Temple in Zhengzhou, China. While working on the special feature for Warner Brothers, I was able to interview David Peterson, a student of Wong Shun Leung's, as part of the documentary. I found David to be a great representative of both the art and his sifu and saw that all the emphasis on Yip Man being Bruce's sole Wing Chun teacher had been misplaced; that Wong had actually been his primary instructor. Consequently, I was inter-

John Little, with the Little Dragon looking over his shoulder. (Photo courtesy of John Little)

ested in learning more about Wong Shun Leung, his role in teaching Bruce Lee, and his own biography as the foremost champion of Yip Man's Wing Chun school. I thought he should be recognized for his contributions not only to Yip Man's art, but also to Bruce Lee's martial development."

In 2010, after almost a decade of holding out, John Little agreed to sell the rights to the Pierre Berton/Bruce Lee interview to Bruce Lee Enterprises, which was now the public face of the Bruce Lee Estate. Not wanting to engage with the estate or its lawyers himself, Little had his business partner, Robert Wolff, handle the transaction.

Almost immediately after divesting himself of the Pierre Berton interview, the lawyers for the Lee Estate withdrew their objections to the Tuttle publishing deal. "As soon as the ink had dried on the agreement," said Little. He resumed receiving his royalties for the Bruce Lee Library series books along with almost a decade of withheld payments.

Looking back, John Little's departure from his role as a Bruce Lee scholar was a major loss for Bruce Lee fans. For the next 20 years, his only contribution to the subject was a small documentary, *Bruce Lee: In Pursuit of the Dragon* (2009), which documented the locations where Bruce Lee shot his films. Little's contributions have been unmatched in the two decades since he resigned.

It was the philosophy of Bruce Lee that suffered most in John Little's absence. "Well, certainly there has been interest in Bruce Lee, and his philosophy," said Little, reflecting on the past efforts to promote Bruce Lee's philosophy and comparing it to the present reality. "I think that has come as a result of the work that we did. Not only Andy, James, and I took it seriously or continued to take it seriously, but certainly gauging by the questions that we received at the universities and among the students of Martin O'Neill, Bruce Lee's philosophy was taken very seriously. We had hoped that it would be the first step; that these philosophical lectures would continue in different countries and help to elevate Bruce's status as a philosopher, perhaps, to those who only thought of him as a martial artist. But I can't say, in all candor, that we made a big impact on that field. I think the big thrust has always been the image of Bruce Lee. So, the movie star or the man who was in these films, and his physical prowess and his fighting ability, are far more marketable things than his thought – despite the fact that it was his thought that informed everything he did, from his acting, to his choreography, to the development of his own martial arts. I know that there has been little

John Little reflecting on his time promoting Bruce Lee's philosophy. (Author's archives)

more mention of Bruce Lee's philosophy since our visit to Ireland, but I don't think anyone has really gone into it as thoroughly as we did at that period of time; and, to this day, they still prefer to focus on Bruce Lee as this physical phenom. But to me, by ignoring his thought, I think you're losing a large part of an audience that might be able to better identify with Bruce because of his views, for example, on racism, that everyone is one family, and before you can be a white American or Chinese American or Chinese person or a Japanese person, you first had to embrace your humanity. You're a human being, first of all. And then if you're so inclined, if you want to demarcate yourself with those distinctions, that's up to you. But I think the common denominator of our humanity, which is what he stressed, is important. It's still important now. But I don't see anyone really stepping up to, you know, emphasize that."

For nearly a decade, John Little dedicated himself completely to giving Bruce Lee a platform to speak for himself, to bring, to public awareness, the philosophical side of Bruce Lee. Little tried to correct the historical record in his literary output. He felt that a great deal of misinformation and misperceptions about Bruce Lee and his art have been perpetuated, even by some of the people who knew him. "Well, I've certainly learned that, even in regards to people who consider themselves experts on Bruce Lee," said Little. "I mean, I enjoyed the interesting perspective of having been an outsider looking in and then, I guess you could say, an insider looking out. I would, like most people, believe what people tell me, especially if there was some connection they may have had with Bruce. If they actually met him, then my first thought was a) they must be telling the truth because why would they lie, and b) they knew Bruce Lee so what possible grounds would they have for distorting the truth. Much like people say, *'Well, it must be true because it's printed in the newspaper.'* Anyone in the newspaper business will tell you that that isn't always the case."

After a two-decade hiatus from writing about Bruce Lee, John Little surprised Lee fans all over the world by releasing the book, *The Wrath of the Dragon: The Real Fights of Bruce Lee* in 2023. The book was written to address the notion that Bruce Lee was not a real fighter. In the book, Little documented the real fights that Bruce Lee had as well as addressed the false claims of his contemporaries.

One of the misperceptions about Bruce Lee that bothers Little the most is the idea that he was just an actor and wasn't the fighter that his legendary status would claim. "All the so-called 'top' martial arts fighters of the time went to him for instruction. Show me another martial artist to whom all the top martial artists go to for instruction. It doesn't happen, and for them to go to a five foot seven and a half-inch, 135-pound practitioner of what they considered to be a 'Chinese' art, they had to be convinced on a physical level that what he had was infinitely superior to what they had, and that usually involved some kind or impromptu sparring session. But now, since Bruce isn't around, they 'just shared ideas'. To me, that's just an insult to the intelligence of the people who speak to them. It's like Michelangelo and all the artwork he did, and someone saying, *'Well, he wasn't really that good. I didn't learn that much from him. We just sort of swapped brush stroke techniques.'* There's no shame in saying Michelangelo taught you something, because his kind does not come around that often. The same can be said for Bruce Lee. It's all ego, for the most part. Unfortunately, most martial artists, in my observation, can't get over that. It's all about who is the toughest guy in the schoolyard, because that's how they sell gym memberships. They don't try to look at it as the martial arts are like a vehicle to get you from the shore of ignorance to the shore of transcendence.

The students suffer for it, and it's obvious the martial artists have suffered for it with their arrested intellectual development."

In comparison, Little said, Bruce Lee was concerned with more important matters. "He wasn't hung up on it. He didn't go around, you know, closing people's schools down, or getting his nose out of joint because someone said something that questioned his talent. He was confident of what he could do and, more to the point, he had moved on from it. He got into film; he was creating new arts of choreography; he was writing screenplays. He wasn't sitting at home stewing about whether or not so-and-so thought he could throw a harder sidekick. If they wanted to know how hard his sidekick was, they knew his number. The irony is that, when he was alive, none of these guys said boo. But when he's dead, then suddenly they're on a par with him."

Despite the difficulties at the end, John Little has fond memories of his time immersed in the words and the world of Bruce Lee. "There were a lot," said Little. "It was a surreal experience in many ways: initially speaking with Linda, meeting Linda, being friends with her was enjoyable at the time. Being left alone at the storage locker with all of Bruce's belongings was both strange and exciting. Even things related to that were enjoyable: transporting the contents of that storage locker to an office unit we had rented. Going through all of the materials, even purchasing bookshelves, assembling them, and putting all of Bruce's books up on those shelves. Spending up to eight hours a day examining his writings, examining his daytime diaries, tacking his big tiger skin up on the wall. This was surreal stuff.

"Then there were the associations and friendships; spending a lot of time with people like Ted Wong, Taky Kimura, Herb Jackson, Jesse Glover, Daniel Lee, and the rest of the Nucleus members was certainly edifying. The Nucleus events were tremendous in that we actually were helping to preserve and perpetuate Bruce's art and philosophy. Getting Bruce's Marcy circuit trainer, and having Ted Wong and Herb Jackson assemble it for me. Again, very surreal stuff for somebody who had been a fan since sitting in the theatre at the age of 12, watching *Enter the Dragon* on the big screen in a theatre in Toronto, Canada. And it was also interesting meeting people who grew up having the same Bruce Lee experience that I did, but from other countries. Also, convincing Warner Brothers to restore the excised footage from *Enter the Dragon* back into the film for the 1998 release, and particularly the monk scene in which

John Little, Martin O'Neill, and Andy Kimura having fun at Trinity College before the Bruce Lee Symposium. (Author's archives)

Bruce espoused more of his personal philosophy."

Asked if he had any regrets, Little smiled and shook his head. "I don't really have any regrets, as I did the best I could during my tenure. I would've liked to have directed the screenplay he wrote, which I came upon amongst his personal papers. I also received another portion of that script that Brandon Lee had and was able to connect the two together to see the full storyline. That excited me for a while. There may have been another book or two that could've been written, but it didn't work out. I don't think I would've done anything differently."

When referred to as the preeminent Bruce Lee scholar, John Little dismissed the idea. "I never considered myself a scholar on the subject," he said. "I was simply the guy that went down into the cave and brought stuff out for people to see. There was no final act or crowning moment. Just an ongoing process of trying to better understand a person that I had been very interested in from a very young age."

Brandon Lee in the movie Rapid Fire. *(Alamy)*

Family

Bruce Lee's son *Brandon Lee* was poised to become an even greater star in Hollywood than his father. He was blessed with his father's good looks and athletic grace, but he was also the image of the all-American boy and may well have been a better actor than his famous father. "Bruce was a martial artist who used his martial arts skills and knowledge to work on perfecting his skills as an actor," said film producer Andre Morgan. "Brandon was an actor who, in the beginning, was not that comfortable with the martial arts and was certainly not comfortable being the son of Bruce Lee on film, because he always wanted to be his own man. He wanted to be Brandon Lee. But as success came to him as an actor, he became more and more comfortable with the idea that you could combine both. It was fascinating to see that turn as he traveled down the road."

After appearing in the *Kung Fu* television reunion movie with David Carradine, Lee spent some time in the East making movies such as *Laser Mission* and *Legacy of Rage,* later graduating into American movies with *Showdown in Little Tokyo* and *Rapid Fire.* Until his life was cut tragically short on March 31, 1993, Brandon Lee's future seemed to have no limits.

"When he went off to make *The Crow,* he was so excited because he felt it was going to be the first movie that really represented Brandon as an actor, as a talent, and would give him his series of movies that he could come back to every couple of years," said Morgan. "I spoke to him the day before he died. He was thrilled with the outcome of that hard work and was really looking forward to finishing the film and going through with his wedding and honeymoon and being back in time to go to the premiere of that film, which he believed would seriously change his career."

Brandon Lee as Eric Draven in The Crow. (Alamy)

Then, on March 31, 1993, shortly after midnight, Brandon Lee was at a Wilmington, North Carolina soundstage where he was filming final scenes for *The Crow*. That night, he was filming a scene in which his character is shot down by a thug. The scene called for the other actor to fire a gun loaded with blanks in Lee's direction, at which point the "bullet wound" effects planted on Brandon's body, or *squibs*, would go off and Lee would fall to the ground as if shot. The director called action, the bad guy discharged the gun, and Lee collapsed to the ground on cue. As the crew patted themselves on the back for a job well done, Brandon Lee did not get up.

The production crew quickly realized the horrible truth.

Lee was rushed to the Hanover Regional Medical Center with an abdominal wound the size of a silver dollar. For five hours, surgeons tried to repair the damage done to his internal organs, eventually transfusing him with 60 pints of blood. They were ultimately unsuccessful.

Brandon Lee died at 1:04 p.m. that afternoon, with his fiancé, Eliza Hutton, at his side. They were to be married a week after filming on *The Crow* was finished.

Immediately, there was a great uproar in the movie industry. There were many unanswered questions. Why wasn't Brandon wearing a protective vest, as was the standard practice when filming such a scene? Why did the actor aim the gun directly at Brandon, when it is customary for actors to aim just to the left or right of their target, for safety's sake? Why did the gun have real bullets in it, and why was the weapons supervisor given the night off? Something was not right, and people wanted immediate answers. Fellow actor and martial artist Steven Seagal went on record about the incident, saying: "Something is terribly wrong here."

Conspiracy nuts were quick to call it a clandestine affair. The old rumors of murder associated with Bruce Lee's death resurfaced for Brandon Lee's passing. Tales of "curses" surrounding the Bruce Lee family also were resurrected, as if Brandon's death were somehow proof of that.

What some people were calling a conspiracy was really nothing more than a series of fatal errors, mistakes, and irresponsible management that culminated in the death of a rising star. The prop gun that fired the fatal shot was previously used for a close up of the discharge. When close ups were filmed of guns, it was customary, at the time, to use a dummy bullet that actually flies out of the barrel, so that the audience can see it. One of these dummy bullets became lodged in the barrel, which would have been discovered had the weapon been properly inspected, and when the gun was reloaded with blanks, the dummy bullet remained inside. As a result, when the actor pulled the trigger, the concussive force of the blank propelled the dummy bullet out of the barrel and into the abdomen of Lee with enough, though not all, of the force of a real bullet.

Since Brandon Lee was filming his final scenes when the accident took place, *The Crow* was able to be completed with stand-ins and minimal CGI. It became a big hit when it was released, proving to be the breakthrough role for Lee that *Enter the Dragon* was for his father. Like Bruce Lee, Brandon Lee left us too soon.

Three weeks after the death of Brandon Lee, his sister, Shannon Lee, his mother, Linda Lee Cadwell, Brandon Lee's fiancé, Eliza Hutton, and Bruce Lee's brother, Robert Lee, attend the Hollywood Walk of Fame Ceremony for Bruce Lee on April 28, 1993 at 6933 Hollywood Boulevard in Hollywood, California. (Photo by Barry King/Alamy Stock Photo)

On April 28, 1993, Bruce Lee received his star on the Hollywood Walk of Fame. His widow, Linda Lee Cadwell, and his daughter, Shannon, accepted it on his behalf. The ceremony drew thousands of people, including *Enter the Dragon* producer Fred Weintraub, Bruce Lee's brother, Robert Lee, and martial arts action star Jean-Claude Van Damme.

It was a bittersweet moment for the Lee family. With the recent death of her son foremost on her mind, Linda Lee Cadwell turned an acceptance speech into an impassioned platform for change. "Bruce Lee envisioned his dreams and made them come true. I feel I represent Bruce Lee here today, and if he were here, he would want to say to the film community that something like Brandon's death must never happen again. So, I am calling for positive action to the film community, individually and collectively, to take measures that safety precautions they have on their film set will never lead to this series of negligent acts that took the life of my son."

Linda Lee Cadwell and her daughter, Shannon Lee, visiting the gravesites of Bruce and Brandon Lee at Lakeview Cemetery in Seattle. (Author's archives)

With the loss of Brandon Lee, the eyes of Bruce Lee fans everywhere turned to Bruce Lee's daughter, Shannon. *Shannon Lee* (who graduated with a Bachelor of Fine Arts in Vocal Performance from Tulane University) was just beginning to explore a career as an actress (having appeared in a cameo role in *Dragon: The Bruce Lee Story*) when her brother was killed.

Growing up, Shannon Lee had little interest in martial arts. As a child, she trained briefly with Bruce Lee student Richard Bustillo, but quit because of comparisons made to her father.

She did, however, see herself becoming an actor or a singer. "I didn't want to seem like I was jumping on the bandwagon," said Shannon Lee in a February 1994 interview in *Black Belt* magazine, "but acting is a genuine interest of mine and something I've wanted to do for a long time. If the acting thing or the singing thing don't pan out, I won't be crushed, I don't think."

In that same interview, she dismissed the idea of doing martial arts movies. "No, I wouldn't. A couple of times, people would ask, *'Wouldn't you want to do a martial arts film?'* And I'd say, *'Well, I don't do martial arts. I'd be a complete fraud.'* And that's not what I'm out to be."

She spoke about her desire to be an actress with her brother, Brandon, shortly before he died. "He sort of encouraged and discouraged me at the same time, saying it was a hard profession and one gets a lot of rejection, and being a woman, I would be objec-

Shannon Lee in her first starring role as "Mi Lo" with Lou Ferrigno as "Billy" in Cage II: Arena of Death. *The film also starred Bruce Lee's friend, Leo Fong, as "Tanaka".* (United Archives GmbH / Alamy Stock Photo)

tified," she said. "But if I really wanted to do it, he would help and support me any way he could. But then he had his accident, so it was hard and slow for me to get into it."

Shannon eventually made it into films, beginning with *Cage II: Arena of Death,* which co-starred Lou Ferrigno and her father's friend, Leo Fong. Her first real movie was a challenge for Shannon Lee, because the script called for her character, Mi Lo, to be struck by a bullet. On the day of filming, Lee began to panic at the thought of filming a scene that paralleled her own brother's tragic death. "She was crying, really upset about the idea that a prop gun would be pointed at her," said Ferrigno. "She was hysterical. We could understand why."

While initially reluctant to cash in on her family's association with martial arts, Shannon Lee seemed to change her mind once she began acting. She hosted 1990s series *WMAC Masters,* a show about a fictional martial arts competition; as the on-camera host, she was not required to perform any martial arts. Lee left the show after the first season.

Around the same time, Lee began training in martial arts to secure film roles. She took lessons in kickboxing with Benny Urquidez, Taekwondo with Tan Tao-Liang, Wushu with Eric Chen, and additional theatrical martial arts training with Yuen De. According to Bruce Lee student Ted Wong, Shannon Lee also received private instruction in Jeet Kune Do from Wong on three separate occasions.

Lee's next movie was *High Voltage.* After *High Voltage,* Lee worked on the film *Enter the Eagles* co-starring Benny Urquidez. She also had a small cameo as a medical resident in the first two minutes of the vampire movie, *Blade.*

In 1998, Warner Brothers and WB TV announced the development of an action comedy/drama series starring Shannon Lee. Lee's character was described as a single woman who worked as a spy. The announcement of the series, and Shannon Lee's role in it, triggered a negative response from a group composed primarily of Hollywood stuntwomen and female martial artists who took offense to the public promotion of non-martial art actresses (such as Lucy Lawless in *Xena: Warrior Princess* and Sarah Michelle-Gellar in *Buffy: The Vampire Slayer*) as actual martial artists. Calling themselves the *Martial Arts Net Surfers,* the group placed a full-page advertisement in the May 11, 1998 edition of *Daily Variety.* The advertisement was an open letter to Warner Brothers.

> "Your plan is to exploit Bruce Lee's name to promote a series which features a non-martial artist doing imitation Jackie Chan-style fighting (using stunt doubles of course). Your 'star', Shannon Lee, Bruce Lee's daughter, is not a martial artist (to call her a neophyte would be a compliment) nor is she an accomplished actor or comedian. There is only one reason you are doing a series featuring her – her name. Your plan is to milk the goodwill and respect that young people have for Bruce Lee and our attraction for Jackie Chan's comedic style fighting. But your strategy to cash in on our heroes will surely backfire."

The group called on Warner Brothers to reconsider their plans. "We have no problem with deception and illusion within the context of a movie," said a spokesperson for the group. "What we're criticizing is the deception in the context of real-life relationships, specifically the relationship between the actor and the public. This dishonesty and deception is a problem because it's against core martial arts principles and serious martial arts advocates, like Bruce Lee, who embody these principles."

Whether it was in response to the public criticism or some unrelated reason, WB TV canceled development of the series.

Shannon Lee made a total of six films in which she had a significant role. Her last film, *Lessons for an Assassin,* was released in 2003. That same year, Shannon Lee provided vocals and co-wrote songs for the pop band Medicine's album, *The Mechanical Forces of Love.* The album was well-received by critics; *The Guardian* gave it four out of five stars, calling Lee's voice "extraordinary" and that it "floats past like clouds or flutters down as if it had been chopped up in a blender."

After the release of *Lessons for an Assassin,* Shannon Lee stepped back from acting, focusing her energies on her roles as a new mother and caretaker of the Bruce Lee Estate and Bruce Lee Enterprises. In her role as the head of Bruce Lee Enterprises, she manages the licensing of Bruce Lee's image and name and promotes the brand through social media, podcasts, and merchandising on the official website. She also manages the archives of the Bruce Lee Estate, which includes Bruce Lee's writings.

In 2019, Shannon Lee was credited as a producer of the Cinemax television series, *Warrior.* Executive produced by Justin Lin and created by Jonathan Tropper, the series is based on Bruce Lee's unproduced treatment for a martial arts television series set among the Tong Wars of the late 1800s. The series lasted for three seasons and a total of 30 episodes. Shannon Lee returned to acting for a one-episode appearance in the final season.

WHAT IF BRUCE LEE HAD LIVED?

Like everyone else, you want to learn the way to win, but never to accept the way to lose. To accept defeat – to learn to die – is to be liberated from it. Once you accept, you are free to flow and harmonize. Fluidity is the way to an empty mind. So when tomorrow comes, you must free your ambitious mind and learn the art of dying.

Bruce Lee

What if Bruce Lee had lived? It is the question that his fans and friends continually ask themselves. Lee died well before he could accomplish all of his goals. It is a double tragedy when someone with so much potential dies early. Not only do you lose a life, but you also lose the positive things they could have accomplished. Bruce Lee had many dreams left to realize.

Lee planned to move back to the United States permanently after the success of *Enter the Dragon*. He felt that, to grow as an actor, he would have to establish himself in the United States. He thought that, once he did, he could progress into roles that did not just trade on his martial arts prowess. "I would like to evolve into different roles, but I cannot do so in Southeast Asia. I am already being typecast." Lee said that he was unable to fully express himself in Asian films because the public always demanded that he play the same character, the stalwart hero who had no personal deficiencies and, consequently, little depth.

Conversely, Bruce Lee felt that the United States had the wrong image of Asia and that he could, through his films, open the eyes of America to the beauty of the Orient. In 1971, he said, "I have already made up my mind that in the United States something about the Oriental, *I mean the true Oriental,* should be shown."

Lee felt that the Orient needed an education, too. "I believe that I have a role here in Southeast Asia. The audience needs to be educated, and the one to educate them has to be someone responsible. We are dealing with the masses, and we have to create something that will get through to them. We have to educate them step by step. We can't do it overnight. That's what I am doing now. Whether I succeed or not remains to be seen. But I don't just *feel* committed, I *am* committed."

Cinema

According to his fans, Bruce Lee, had he lived, would find himself teaming up with some of the biggest names in the movie business. And, of course, there would be two more members of the Lee family making movies by this time. "At this point, I think he'd be doing some joint ventures with Brandon and Shannon," said fan John Drake. "Perhaps he'd be doing some work with Jackie Chan, only at more of an 'equals' level than just Jackie being the guy that got his neck broke in *Enter the Dragon*. Oh, and definitely some more work with Bolo Yeung!"

"I think Bruce would have expanded his work in movies more than anything," said Jeet Kune Do practitioner Andy Wilson. "I think he would have had a few more hit movies in the martial arts genre; then, I suspect, he'd want to go into some straight action and drama movies. I guess he would've hit a roadblock with his mainstream potential as a leading man in the USA."

"I believe Bruce Lee would have enjoyed the success he received for *Enter the Dragon,* which would have moved him into a position in the film industry whereby he could choose what projects he wanted to be involved in and with whom he wanted to work," said Chris Kent. "I think he would have continued in his film career as an actor as well as moving more into writing, directing, and producing, making both action films and films with deeper meaning behind them."

Bruce Lee authority John Little agrees with Chris Kent that Bruce Lee would have increasingly focused more on directing. "Undoubtedly, he would've grabbed as much of the money that was offered him by various production companies after *Enter Dragon* was released," said Little. "He always wanted to be a multimillionaire and a huge movie star; he worked hard at putting himself in a position where he could achieve this, and so it is unlikely that, once in that position, he would refuse it. There is some evidence that he was getting picky about his image, and the projects that he would appear in, which might have factored into his decisions. I suspect that he would have made a bunch of movies, made a lot of money, and then stepped behind the camera to direct. He may, like Steve McQueen, have created his own production company and worked on co-producing feature films."

Had Bruce Lee lived, one tantalyzing possibility is that he would have participated in the Star Wars franchise. (James Bishop/Midjourney AI)

One of the more interesting predictions for Bruce Lee's cinema career came from Ric Meyers, an author and Hong Kong Cinema action expert. Meyers suggested that Lee would have been a natural for the role of Lord of the Jedi Knights in George Lucas' Star Wars prequels. Or, perhaps, a role not unlike Donnie Yen's character in *Rogue One: A Star Wars Story*.

Martial Arts

In his martial arts, Bruce Lee accepted the reality that his skills and attributes would diminish over time. When asked whether he would still be the same fighter at middle age, Lee's reply was pragmatic. "The man himself will not realize it and will probably deny it. But physiologically, he is already on the decline, and I think the fighter over 45 should sit back and watch the emergence of the new ones."

At the same time, Lee felt that he would gain in other areas. He noted that his teacher had developed an unusually keen sense of intuition in his old age. "I expect that my awareness will increase as did my instructor's, Yip Man."

It is possible, too, that once his physical attributes started to decline and he could no longer be so elusive, Bruce Lee would begin placing more emphasis on grappling techniques – more so than he had in his prime. He realized that he would not be the same man that he was before, and that he would have to change to accept his current situation, a very Taoist concept. A hint to how he might have approached his martial art at middle age is found in some advice he gave author Joe Hyams. "Stop comparing yourself at 45 with the man you were at 20 or 30. The past is an illusion. You must learn to live in the present and accept yourself for what you are now. What you lack in flexibility and agility, you must make up with knowledge and constant practice."

Patrick Strong, who had the distinction of studying with Bruce Lee at both the earlier stages of Lee's martial art development in Seattle and during his final years of development in California, agrees that Lee would have delved more deeply into grappling. Strong also says that Lee intended to continue his studies in Wing Chun. "Just before his death, Bruce felt the strong need to improve his grounding and the ability to hold pressure. He was hoping to

Tokyo, Japan. 20th Apr, 1995. Rickson Gracie, Yoshihisa Yamamoto MMA: Vale Tudo Japan at Nippon Budokan in Tokyo, Japan (Yukio Hiraku/AFLO/Alamy Live News)

get this from Yip Man. Had he lived, I believe that he would have modified his method, as he always did anyway. Certainly, he would have expanded more into ground fighting, possibly becoming best friends with either the Gracies or Machados, or both."

Having studied Ju Jitsu with the Gracie family for a few years, Strong thinks that Bruce Lee would have a great deal in common with Rickson Gracie, in particular. He feels that the two would have developed a lasting friendship based on mutual respect. "In doing so, Bruce would have no doubt made changes to his overall fight strategy. This, in itself, falls into line with his desire to greater strengthen certain aspects of his Wing Chun.

"I can easily see where he would omit a few things to keep up with the ever-evolving martial arts revolution. He would have loved NHB (no-holds barred tournaments), and it would have really gotten his creative juices flowing."

"If Mito Uyehara is to be believed," said John Little, "Bruce would've opened a martial arts school that embodied the latter-day principles of Jeet Kune Do. That is, that the students would go through the same self-educational process he did, but rather than obtaining this knowledge through books and developing friendships with practitioners of other arts, the practitioners of these arts would be brought to the school to present the principles and certain techniques of their arts, which Bruce's students could then decide to adopt (if their attributes allowed) or to reject."

Not everyone agrees that Bruce Lee would broaden the accessibility of Jeet Kune Do. "First and foremost, I think one needs to look at the full trajectory of Bruce's evolution and his vision regarding his art – from his initial idea of creating the *ultimate fighting system* to the concept of the *style-less style* and complete freedom for the individual," said Chris Kent. "The reason for this is that many people have stopped at the ultimate fighting system point, and that's what they promote and teach. And I understand that, because that's a much easier thing to do, especially to the masses. How does one teach such esoteric concepts as complete freedom from styles to the average layperson?

"The prime thing with regard to how Jeet Kune Do would have changed, had Bruce lived, I believe, is that the vast majority of the people training in and teaching Jeet Kune Do today wouldn't be doing so. The one thing I can say with any degree of certainty at all is that Jeet Kune Do was Bruce Lee's art and he definitely would have remained in control of anything and everything related to it, the teaching of it, and the dissemination of information regarding it. I cannot say that it would have remained a 'backyard art' as some people like to believe it should be, but control of the quality of the art would have been closely monitored by Bruce Lee, which would have precluded the notion of having numerous Jeet Kune Do schools everywhere."

Lee's student, Larry Hartsell, went further, suggesting that Bruce Lee would retire the name *Jeet Kune Do*. "I think he would have been progressing Jeet Kune Do and the martial arts. Even drop the name Jeet Kune Do. I know he wanted to pursue every angle of the martial arts, every angle of self-defense, bodybuilding, conditioning, and everything else. So, I think he would have been into a lot of the weaponry, the Filipino martial arts as well. He was a very gifted person, so he could have probably achieved any goal he wanted."

A number of fans and Jeet Kune Do practitioners agree with Hartsell that Bruce Lee would drop the name of his martial art. "I feel that Bruce would have discarded the name Jeet Kune Do and closed all schools," said Jesus Santiago. "Bruce Lee was a man who didn't want others to copy him; he wanted others to research and express themselves in their own martial arts. Bruce would not have wanted this new classical mess."

Regardless of whether Lee retained the name of his art, some Jeet Kune Do practitioners believe that any changes to Bruce Lee's art would be measured.

"Of course, this is just my opinion, but yes, I feel Bruce Lee would have progressed in his understanding of fighting and the strategies and principles that are inherent to it," said Jeet Kune Do instructor Sean Madigan. "Would his technique change? No, not really. Would the way he used his technique change? Yes, I feel that that this is where the biggest developments would come from. It is the how and the *when* and the *why* of his techniques that may have changed. I do not feel that a great deal of effort would have been put on adding new techniques to his repertoire. I do feel that he would have evolved with the times and adapted new training methods to increase the effectiveness of his fighting method."

"I suspect he'd have relaxed on the idea of creating the 'ultimate fighting method' for himself and settled into a more personal maintenance/discovery/health stage and be focused on other things," said Andy Wilson. "I'd see him moving more and more away from being 'the best' and explored other creative endeavors."

Bruce Lee told Chuck Norris (seen here with Lee and *Way of the Dragon* co-star Nora Miao) that he planned to take 10 years off and then reemerge to see what he could do for the world. (Photo courtesy of the *South China Morning Post*)

"I believe he would really be into all of the recent developments in the fields of fitness and nutrition," said Lamar Davis. "He might have his own line of training equipment, training clothes and instructional videos and motivational tapes. Possibly even his own TV show, where he would cover martial arts, fitness, and nutrition tips. I feel that he would probably put on a little more weight, all *muscle* of course! He would probably be a very big name in the movie industry and, having been extremely successful, take on a major project every two or three years. I think his lifestyle would have evened out a lot and he would take his time with everything, having already accomplished way more than what was stated as *'My Definite Chief Aim'* many, many years before. I think that he would be teaching, but only privately and to close friends whose company he enjoyed. There would be several Jeet Kune Do schools being operated by people whom he had personally trained. With seminars being what they are today, if he would do seminars, he would be, by far, the most demanded seminar instructor on the circuit!"

Philosophy

Bruce Lee felt that he could expand upon his fame and his role as a teacher to bring together nations. British broadcaster Ted Thomas said that Lee told him he hoped to "bring people together."

Perhaps the best hint to what Lee wanted to accomplish was found in the words he wrote to friend Pearl Tso: "I'd like to let the world know about the greatness of this Chinese art (gung fu); I enjoy teaching and helping people; I'd like to have a well-to-do home for my family; I'd like to originate something."

According to Chuck Norris, Bruce Lee planned on retiring around 1975-1976 and then spend 10 years enjoying his family; after which he would reemerge in the public eye to serve in some philanthropic capacity.

Lee felt that there was a dynamic power working in him, pushing him to achieve something. It is very likely that Bruce Lee would have gone on to gain a following as a philosopher and speaker in the vein of Krishnamurti, whose philosophical work he admired and emulated. As a young man, Bruce Lee spent a considerable amount of time exploring the ideas of other philosophers and thinkers. Perhaps, in time, Bruce Lee's own philosophical ideas would have coalesced into a conceptual framework that made them distinctive and appropriate for examination in the fields of philosophy,

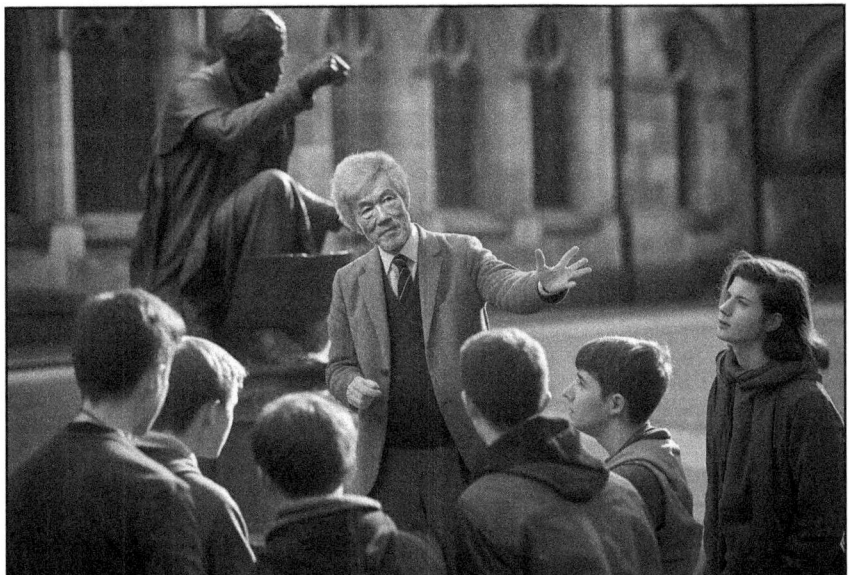

In the future, had Bruce Lee lived, he may have carved out a reputation as a philosopher and public thinker. (James Bishop/Midjourney AI)

psychology, and sociology.

Undoubtedly, though, Bruce Lee's passion for philosophy would remain a core component of his personality. "He probably would have continued to study and apply philosophy," said John Little, "although which flavor of it is hard to know."

Public Service

Lee wanted to have a positive impact on people's lives. He felt that just being a martial arts celebrity was not reason enough to be remembered in the years to come. For a man to truly deserve that kind of immortality, he must change the world for the better.

Is it possible that Bruce Lee would have considered politics? Though he was not interested in politics at the time of his death, that could have changed in the years that followed, as he sought ways in which he could make a difference in the world. He was accustomed to the politics of the martial arts community, which is little different than the politics of government. His abrupt honesty would have been a welcome change from the double-speak and lies of Capitol Hill. Lee's good friend and Taekwondo master Jhoon Rhee had deep ties to the powers-that-be in Washington DC, instructing many members of congress in the martial arts. Another person Lee

Is it possible that Bruce Lee would consider a run for United States president? (James Bishop/Midjourney AI)

knew, Gary Locke, went on to become the first Chinese-American governor in the United States (Washington State). Lee's widow, Linda Lee Cadwell, stated that it was always his intention to return to Seattle and live there, where he would have likely renewed his friendship with Locke. Considering these factors, it would not be a stretch to imagine that Lee would be bumping elbows with government officials who might see his rapport with people and his celebrity as strengths that could help a potential candidate. It must also be remembered that Lee was a United States citizen by birth and was qualified to run for president of the United States despite his being raised in Hong Kong, provided he lived in the country for a specified period prior to his running. Though it is unlikely Bruce Lee would have considered running for the highest seat in the land, it is an intriguing thought.

One thing is certain: Bruce Lee was not planning to die in 1973. He had too much to do, too much for which to live. Shortly before his death, he told his brother that he intended to live to be 100 years old. Lee envisioned himself like the Taoist priest in *Enter the Dragon*. "If you ask me what I will do in Heaven," said Bruce Lee, "I will say this: *'There are many things in this life I have not finished. Why should I think about something so far away?'"*

OUT OF THE DARKNESS OF OUR OWN IGNORANCE

When you're faced with looking at your own life with awakened eyes, you will have increased a bit in the knowledge of yourself and knowledge of anything outside of yourself is only superficial and very shallow. To put it another way, self-knowledge has a liberating quality.

Bruce Lee

When I interviewed author John Little for this book, he made a comparison of Bruce Lee's teachings and efforts to liberate people's minds to Plato's *Allegory of the Cave*. I believe he made a profound and fit comparison. In the *Allegory of the Cave,* the philosopher describes a dark cave where people have been chained up since childhood. They are forced to face the wall of the cave and have never seen the fire burning behind them or the people passing by. The only knowledge they have is of the shadows cast against the wall. These prisoners are forced into a state of perpetual ignorance.

Bruce Lee felt that people in today's society were experiencing a similar sort of bondage. "Styles tend to separate men, because they have their own doctrines and then the doctrines become the gospel truth that you cannot change!" In our world today, we simply accept what we are told to believe at face value without examining its root or the ideology and motivation behind it. Too often, we are getting a partial or imperfect piece of the "truth" that excludes something vital.

Bruce Lee believed in our inherent right to question the status quo and to pursue knowledge with a critical and investigative eye. He believed that an inner change was needed for society to evolve. Social change outwardly will always fail so long as there is no inner change, no revolution within each and every one of us.

A perfect example of Bruce Lee's influence on societies and cultures can be found in the efforts of Martin O'Neill, a social worker and Jeet Kune Do instructor in Belfast, Northern Ireland. During the sectarianism of the Troubles, Northern Ireland was a hotbed of political violence and religious and cultural animosity. There was a deeply ingrained hatred between the Catholic and Protestant groups, which dates back nearly 300 years. At that time, much blood was shed over these people's differences. Using Bruce Lee's example and his martial art of Jeet Kune Do, O'Neill was able to bring together divided Irish who thought they could never be friends and show them that "under the sky, under the heavens, there is but one family."

"It's a society at war with itself," said O'Neill. "There's a lot of hatred that goes on in this society. The hatred here in Ireland knows no bounds in many ways. It's a very sad indictment of our inability to live together. I suppose it has parallels to some of the kind of racism we find in all societies, and I think America has its fair share of that. The book *The Warrior Within* had a chapter on racism and Bruce Lee's experiences with racism, which I really related to in terms of the experiences I have had of sectarianism (which is like a parallel of racism) in terms of my religion because you're condemned in my society and labeled as an accident of birth as to whether you're born a Protestant or Catholic."

At his Jun Fan/Jeet Kune Do school in Belfast, O'Neill was able to bring together Catholics and Protestants under one roof and unite them under the common thread of Bruce Lee's teachings and philosophies. "All I can do is make a small contribution to the peace process, and I do that through my community relations work and through my involvement with Jeet Kune Do, by saying that Jeet Kune Do is open to everyone and the door is open. Because Bruce's art transcends color or creed, people can come in and learn, grow together, and develop friendships. And that's very important, I think."

O'Neill said he is grateful to be able talk to and learn from so

Martin O'Neill meeting Taky Kimura in 1999. (Author's archives)

many people who knew Bruce Lee. In 1999, he had the opportunity to speak to Taky Kimura at Bruce Lee's gravesite. "Meeting Taky Kimura all those years ago at Bruce Lee's gravesite at Lakeview Cemetery in Seattle was a memorable experience. He's a brilliant man. Taky came over and spoke to me about Bruce. I was amazed that he was so friendly and willing to talk about what Bruce meant to him. He spoke to me the way you would speak to a friend. He's a very open person and someone who cares."

After meeting Taky Kimura and his son, Andy, in 1999, Martin O'Neill became an instructor under the Kimura lineage.

"Being a friend, student, and instructor with Taky and Andy has been a real honor for me, as they represent what Bruce Lee stood for: honor, integrity, and truth," said O'Neill. "Being a part of the Jun Fan Gung Fu Institute family has allowed me to meet people from all over the world and make friends and connections within and beyond martial arts. For me, martial arts are a means of personal challenge and growth as a human being, and I remain eternally grateful for the guidance and support from Sigung Taky, Sifu Andy, and their family over the years."

O'Neill's experiences with the Bruce Lee legacy are something he will treasure forever. "Life is a journey rather than a destination. The destination is when we die. We might have the big destination then, but certainly my journey has been enriched by having an opportunity to train in Bruce Lee's art."

"A lot of things you take for granted," said John Little. "There's so many, his (Bruce's) teachings cover such a broad field. The whole idea of not accepting tradition for tradition's sake. Accept it if there is a reason for it, but you must know what the reason is; not to be part of a herd mentality, which is very important. Development of the individual character, as opposed to meek complacency."

Alex Shunnarah, a Jeet Kune Do practitioner in Florida, said Bruce Lee's martial art has done more for him than simply develop his fighting skills. "Jeet Kune Do has liberated me from mental anguish and stress. Simply put, it has given me a new lease on life."

Most importantly, Bruce Lee teaches us that we are only limited by how much we believe in ourselves. You may set out on the same road with a greater distance to cover than someone else, but you may both reach the same destination, if you are willing to work for it.

"As I look back, I realize what Bruce imparted in me was not totally about physical combat, it was about life," said Leo Fong. "I get a sense that what he said had martial arts implications, but the bottom line was that it went beyond that. It went deeper. Anyone who can break through the boundaries of physical combat will understand that Jeet Kune Do has to do with handling life's situations. I got a glimpse of that when he said, *'I practice martial arts so I can knock the hell out of my fears and insecurities.'* The insightful person will see the spiritual and mental dimension of the Bruce Lee concepts. It's easy to punch out an attacker. It takes more than physical skill to overcome the loss of a loved one to terminal illness, facing death, divorce, and other adversities. What Bruce showed me and taught me was the need to develop inner strength and self-reliance.

"In an excellent article written in the September 1971 issue of *Black Belt* magazine, titled 'Liberate Yourself from Classical Karate', Bruce talked about confinement. He said, *'One cannot express himself fully when imprisoned by a confined style. Lacking boundaries, combat is always fresh, alive, and constantly changing.'* After going into details about Jeet Kune Do and how much different his approach is compared to the classical styles, Bruce said, *'At this point you may ask how do I gain this knowledge? That you have to find out all by yourself. You must accept the fact that there is no help but self-help. For the same reason, I cannot tell you how to gain freedom, since freedom exists within you.'*

"It is my belief that the highest compliment we can pay to Bruce Lee is not to try to be a clone of Bruce, but rather take that which is good, which he had left to us, and discover the truth within."

Bruce Lee: warrior, philosopher, teacher, and friend (1940-1973). (Photo courtesy of Globe Photos, Inc.)

"There's nothing that Bruce Lee accomplished that is beyond the realm of anyone if they are willing to put forth the will to do it," said John Little. "You don't know what your limitations are. That is something that can only be accurately accessed in retrospect, so you never know how good you're going to be or what you can accomplish until you put forth the effort to try it."

Taky Kimura, who passed away in 2021 at the age of 96, saw the effect that Bruce Lee had on people every time he went to Lakeview Cemetery to tend to Bruce Lee's grave. "I go up to the cemetery all the time and I see these people up there and many of them aren't even martial artists, but they're up there. They're up there looking for something within themselves. When you look at all these people out there who claim that they aren't role models, they are role models, because they are in the limelight. But Bruce is a guy who inspires others. Even decades later, that cemetery is so trodden that they just put new sod up there. You watch, in a few months it will be worn out again. When I go up there, I usually bump into somebody. I try not to be forward, but I usually introduce myself. I ask them why they are up there, and they tell me these things, you know, and it's just incredible the inspiration Bruce is creating, aiding these people."

Without a doubt, Bruce Lee was an unparalleled dynamo of cinematic majesty and martial art virtuosity. But Lee's true legacy is not in the films he made or the martial art he founded; his real legacy is in the family, students, friends, and fans who were inspired by Lee to liberate themselves and achieve their own greatness. That is why Bruce Lee matters, and that is why his legacy and inspiration will endure.

APPENDIX

Recommended Resources

The following is a list of recommended books, websites, and museums to continue your study of Bruce Lee, his martial art, philosophy, and teachings.

Books

The Bruce Lee Library Series

Words of the Dragon
by Bruce Lee; edited by John Little
The Tao of Gung Fu
by Bruce Lee; edited by John Little
Jeet Kune Do: Commentaries on the Martial Way
by Bruce Lee; edited by John Little
The Art of Expressing the Human Body
by Bruce Lee; edited by John Little
Letters of the Dragon
by Bruce Lee; edited by John Little
Artist of Life
by Bruce Lee; edited by John Little
Striking Thoughts
by Bruce Lee; edited by John Little

Books on Jeet Kune Do

Tao of Jeet Kune Do
by Bruce Lee
   A book of Bruce Lee's notes published posthumously.

Who Wrote the Tao? The Literary Sourcebook for the Tao of Jeet Kune Do
by James Bishop
> The ultimate guide to the true sources of the content of the *Tao of Jeet Kune Do*.

The Bruce Lee Fighting Method: Volume One
by Bruce Lee and M. Uyehara
The Bruce Lee Fighting Method: Volume Two
by Bruce Lee and M. Uyehara
The Bruce Lee Fighting Method: Volume Three
by Bruce Lee and M. Uyehara
The Bruce Lee Fighting Method: Volume Four
by Bruce Lee and M. Uyehara

Chinese Gung Fu: The Philosophical Art of Self Defense
by Bruce Lee
> The only book Bruce Lee authored in his lifetime.

Jeet Kune Do Kickboxing
by Chris Kent & Tim Tackett

Jun Fan/Jeet Kune Do: The Textbook
by Chris Kent & Tim Tackett
> Considered one of the best books on Jeet Kune Do.

Wing Chun Kung Fu
by James Yimm Lee/Technical Editor, Bruce Lee

Wing Chun Kung Fu/Jeet Kune Do: A Comparison
by Ted Wong & William Cheung

Jeet Kune Do: Entering to Trapping to Grappling
by Larry Hartsell

Jeet Kune Do Unlimited
by Burton Richardson

The Jeet Kune Do Mindset: Martial Arts Ways for a Better Life
by Martin O'Neill

Jun Fan Gung Fu: Origins & Evolution
by Ryan Ohl
    Exceptionally well-researched and detailed book.

Sijo Bruce Lee: From Classical to Non-Classical
by Gianfranco Mento
    Deep look into the origins of Bruce Lee's martial arts.

Books on Bruce Lee's Philosophy

The Warrior Within
by John Little
    Bruce Lee's philosophy and applying it to your life.

Words from a Master
by Bruce Lee
    A collection of his interviews.

Bruce Lee: Dynamic Becoming
by James Bishop
    A collection of essays and articles, mostly on Bruce Lee's philosophy and writings.

Liberate Yourself! How To Think Like Bruce Lee
by Chris Kent
    The fundamental tenets of Lee's philosophy of self-actualization and personal liberation.

Zen in the Martial Arts
by Joe Hyams
    Hyams recounts his studies under Bruce Lee and others.

Biographies on Bruce Lee

The Bruce Lee Story
by Linda Lee

Bruce Lee: A Life
by Matthew Polly
    One of the best biographies on Bruce Lee.

Unsettled Matters
by Tom Bleecker

Other Related Books

Bruce Lee: The Evolution of a Martial Artist
by Tommy Gong
    Well-researched and accessible overview of Bruce Lee and Jeet Kune Do

Striking Distance: Bruce Lee and the Dawn of Martial Arts in America
by Charles Russo

Wrath of the Dragon: The Real Fights of Bruce Lee
by John Little

Websites

Bruce Lee
    The official site for Bruce Lee Enterprises. Includes the *Bruce Lee Podcast*.
    (www.brucelee.com)

Bruce Lee Foundation
    Non-profit educational initiative.
    (www.bruceleefoundation.org)

Bruce Lee Library Research Project
    A comprehensive virtual museum and database featuring 2,275 items from Bruce Lee's personal library.
    (www.bruceleelibrary.jamecbishop.com)

Bruce Lee Was Here
    Comprehensive timeline of Lee's life.
    (www.bruceleewashere.com)

Bruce Lee Chinese Gung Fu Book
    Well-researched website devoted to Bruce Lee's only self-published book.
    (www.bruceleechinesegungfubook.com)

Sourcing Bruce Lee
>Excellent blog examining the true sources of quotes attributed to Bruce Lee.
>(www.sourcingbrucelee.blogspot.com)

Museums

The Wing Luke Museum
Seattle, Washington
>The permanent repository of the personal library of Bruce Lee.
>(www.wingluke.org)

Chinese Historical Society of America
San Francisco, California
>Currently housing the "We are Bruce Lee" exhibit.
>(www.chsa.org)

Academy Museum of Motion Pictures
Los Angeles, California
>Includes a number of Bruce Lee movie items in its collection.
>(www.academymuseum.org)

Hong Kong Heritage Museum
Hong Kong
>Has recurring Bruce Lee exhibitions.
>(www.hk.heritage.museum)

BIBLIOGRAPHY

Cater, Dave. "Kareem Speaks!" *Inside Kung Fu,* July 1988, p. 63.

Cater, Dave. "Life After Bruce!" *Martial Arts Legends,* June 1994, pp. 118-125.

Chinn, Jeff. "Rare Gathering Remembers Bruce, Brandon." *Martial Arts Legends,* August 1998, pp. 66-70, 114-115.

Colet, Robert. "Krishnamurti: The Spiritual Force behind Bruce Lee." *Inside Kung Fu Presents,* October 1990, pp. 26-29.

Clouse, Robert. *Bruce Lee: The Biography.* Burbank, California. Unique Publications, Inc., 1988.

The Curse of the Dragon. Directed by Tom Kuhn and Fred Weintraub. Warner Brothers Home Video, 1993.

Dorgan, Michael. "Bruce Lee's Toughest Fight." *Official Karate,* July 1980, p. 18.

Dreher, Diane. *The Tao of Inner Peace.* New York, New York. Harper-Perennial, 1991.

"Enter the Hornet: Van Williams Sets the Record Straight." *Grand Royal Magazine,* Fall/Winter 1993, pp. 52-53.

Hyams, Joe. *Zen in the Martial Arts.* New York, New York. Bantam Books. 1982.

Bruce Lee: the Immortal Dragon. Directed by Jude Gerard Prest. A&E Home Video, 1997.

Joseph, Fran. "A JKD Reunion." *Inside Kung Fu Magazine,* July 1988, pp. 49-59, 104.

Kreng, John. "Truth's Pathless Road." *Kung Fu Presents,* August 1998, pp. 26-29, 60-64, 80-83.

Lee, Bruce. *Letters of the Dragon.* Boston, Massachusetts. Tuttle Publishing, 1998.

Lee, Bruce. *The Tao of Jeet Kune Do.* Santa Clarita, California. Ohara Publications, 1975.

Lee, Bruce. *Words From a Master.* Chicago, Illinois. Contemporary Books, 1999.

Lee, Bruce. *Words of the Dragon.* Boston, Massachusetts. Tuttle Publishing. 1997.

Lee, Linda. *The Bruce Lee Story.* Burbank, California. Ohara Publications. 1989.

Lee, Linda. "What Is Jeet Kune Do?" *Inside Kung Fu Magazine,* April 1997, pp. 40-47, 100.

Little, John. "After the Tears: Shannon Lee Reminisces about Brother Brandon and Father Bruce." *Black Belt Magazine,* Feb 1994, 27-32, 120.

Logan, Bey. "Enter the Dragon: What Really Happened Behind the Scenes!" *Martial Arts Legends Presents,* August 1998, pp. 18-32.

Martial Arts Net Surfers. "Open Letter to the WB Network." https://web.archive.org/web/20000606114704/http://members.xoom.com:80/Martial_Arts/letter.htm. *The Martial Arts Net Surfers.* Accessed 5 January 2024.

Nilsson, Thomas. "Training With Bruce Lee." *Black Belt Magazine,* May 1996, pp. 38-43.

Norris, Chuck. *The Secret Power Within.* New York, New York. Little, Brown and Co., 1996.

Russo, Charles. *Striking Distance: Bruce Lee and the Dawn of Martial Arts in America.* University of Nebraska Press, 2016.

Thomas, Bruce. *Bruce Lee: Fighting Spirit.* Berkeley, California. Frog, Ltd., 1994.

Top Fighter. Directed by Toby Russell. Arena Home Video, 1996.

Tyson, Joseph B. *The New Testament and Early Christianity.* New York, New York. Macmillan Publishing Company. 1984.

Uyehara, M. "The Making of Enter the Dragon." *Black Belt Magazine,* December 1997, p. 30.

Webster-Doyle, Dr. Terrence. "Beyond the Fist." *Bruce Lee Jun Fan Jeet Kune Do Magazine,* December 1997, pp. 6-10.

Wing-tsit Chan. *A Sourcebook in Chinese Philosophy.* Princeton, New Jersey. Princeton University Press, 1973.

Wong, Ted. "Ted Wong and the Genesis of Jeet Kune Do." *Bruce Lee Jun Fan Jeet Kune Do Magazine,* February 1998, pp. 5-14.

Index

ABC, 27, 44, 106
Abdul-Jabbar, Kareem, 26, 36, 52, 71, 78, 148
Ali, Muhammad, 24

Baker, Bob, 79
Batman, 26, 43-45, 138
Belfast, Northern Ireland, 151-153, 184
Benn, Jon T., 31, 123-124
Berton, Pierre, 75, 140, 145-146, 154-155, 158, 160
Big Boss, The, 20, 48, 50, 78, 89, 106, 108, 112, 126, 127
Black Belt Magazine, 1, 9, 29, 92, 169, 186
Blakeman, Robert, 115-122, 146
Block, Alex Ben, 51, 148
Blondie, 46
Boxing, 15-16, 24, 32, 37, 87, 95, 101, 128
Bremer, Bob, 38-39, 66, 71, 73-74
Bruce Lee Café and Museum, 123-124
Bruce Lee Educational Foundation, 3-4, 103, 149-152
Bruce Lee Estate, 2, 3, 38, 80-82, 144, 148, 154-160, 172
Bruce Lee Eve, 116-122
Bruce Lee: His Last Days, His Last Nights, 79
Bruce Lee: In Pursuit of the Dragon, 141, 160
Bruce Lee Library Series, The, 9, 141-142, 149, 155, 156, 160,
Bruce Lee: The Lost Interview, 145-146, 154-155, 160
Bruce Lee Magazine, 149
Bruce Lee: The Man Only I Knew, 80-82
Bruce Lee: A Warrior's Journey, 147-148, 150, 151, 153, 155-158
Bustillo, Richard, 90, 169

Cadwell, Linda Lee, 2-5, 21-22, 33-34, 52, 53, 59, 61-66, 71, 76, 78-82, 104, 109-110, 142-146, 151, 153, 155, 163, 168, 169
Cage II: The Arena of Death, 170-171
Cannabis (marijuana; hashish), 79, 80
Carradine, David, 46, 106, 165
Chan, Jackie, 58, 60, 172, 174
Charlie Chan, 43
Chinn, Jeff, 105-111
China, 21, 49, 51, 53, 158
Chinese Gung Fu: The Philosophical Art of Self-Defense, 34
Chinese Opera, 11
Chow, Raymond, 47-48, 50, 59-60, 78, 80
Chow, Ruby, 15-16
Clouse, Robert, 53, 56, 60
Coburn, James, 26, 76, 79
Cocaine, 79
Cohen, Rob, 82
Cole, Mark, 80

Colosseum, 51
Concord Productions, 50
Confucius, 33, 34, 42, 75
Crow, The, 166-167

Davis II, Lamar, 92-93, 99, 103, 178-180
Dean, James, 77
Deery, Jim, 152-153
DeMile, James, 15-16, 17
Dempsey, Jack, 24

Dozier, William, 43-46, 63
Dragon: The Bruce Lee Story, 6-8, 82, 169
Dreher, Diane, 42,
Dublin, Ireland, 125, 130, 132-135, 139, 151, 153
Durant, Will, 158

Easy Rider, 127
Edison Technical High School, 15
Edwards, Blake, 28
Elms, Gary, 13
Emerald City Productions, 132-134
Enter the Dragon, 32, 52-60, 73, 75-76, 80, 88, 107-108, 110, 115, 127, 146, 163, 167, 168, 173, 174, 175, 182
Enter the Eagles, 171

Fair City, 136-139
Fencing, 24, 25, 37, 128, 133
Fist of Fury, 49-50, 75, 78, 79, 126, 127
Fong, Leo, 36, 38, 170-171, 186
Fox, Carl, 154
Franciscus, James, 40, 47

Game of Death, 52, 60, 84, 147-148
Glover, Jesse, 163
Golden, Steve, 2, 32, 102-103, 109
Golden Gate Girl, 11
Golden Harvest, 47-50, 80, 147
Gracie, Rickson, 176-177
Green Hornet, The, 26-28, 32, 44-47, 59, 64, 73, 79, 90, 92, 106, 115
Gung Fu, 13-14, 15-23, 34, 36, 61-62, 64, 67, 75, 84, 87, 89, 90, 101, 107-108, 110, 124, 180, 185

Hanley, Joe, 125-140
Hart, Ed, 16, 20, 85
Hartsell, Larry, 2, 29, 32, 69, 73, 85-87, 94, 97, 104, 118, 178
Heller, Paul, 57
Here Comes the Brides, 46
High Voltage, 171
Ho, Grace, 11, 14
Hollywood, 26, 44, 46, 50, 52, 64, 79, 80, 111, 165, 168, 171
Hong Kong, 11-14, 43, 46-51, 53, 55, 59, 63-64, 71, 73, 74, 75, 77-79, 82, 85, 123-124, 157, 175, 182
Hung, Sammo, 32, 59,
Hyams, Joe, 40, 176

India, 36
Inosanto, Dan, 9, 20-21, 24, 40, 41, 52, 69, 76, 83-84, 85, 89-91, 94, 96, 103-104
Inside Kung Fu magazine, 1, 110
Ironside, 46

Jacobs, Pete, 109
Jackson, Herb, 28, 163
Japan, 40, 49, 86, 176
Jeet Kune Do, 2-3, 8, 10, 23, 25, 26, 29-30, 34, 36, 38, 47, 54, 63, 76, 81, 82, 84, 89-104, 128, 140, 144, 148-149, 155, 171, 174, 176-178, 184, 186
Joe, Allen, 109
Johnson, Gilbert, 81
Judo, 31, 101, 127, 128
Ju Jitsu, 91, 177
Jun Fan Gung Fu, 19, 21, 84, 89, 90
Jun Fan Gung Fu Institute, 21, 185
Jun Fan Jeet Kune Do, 2, 101-104, 149
Jun Fan Jeet Kune Do Nucleus, 101-104, 109, 148-149, 155, 184
Juno and the Paycock, 134

Karate, 6, 17-18, 20, 24, 26, 28, 49, 101, 112, 127-130, 132, 141
Kennedy, John F., 77
Kenpo Karate, 20-21, 50, 85, 99, 101, 127-133
Kent, Chris, 109, 155-156, 174, 177
Kimura, Andy, 151, 160, 164, 185
Kimura, Taky, 2, 16-20, 26, 34, 64, 67-69, 76, 88, 109, 151, 163, 185, 188
Krishnamurti, Jiddu, 36-38, 41, 150, 180
Kung Fu, 5, 13, 34, 44, 49, 106, 109, 118, 120, 126, 127, 158
Kung Fu (television series), 46, 70, 106, 165

Lao Tzu, 33-36, 40-42
LaSalle College, 13, 145
LeBell, Gene, 31
Lee, Brandon Bruce, 3, 63-66, 78, 140,

142, 164-169, 174
Lee, Daniel, 2, 36, 163
Lee, George, 2, 109
Lee, Greglon, 63
Lee Hoi Chuen, 11
Lee, James Yimm, 19, 21-23, 62-64, 101
Lee, Jason Scott, 82
Lee, Linda, 2-5, 21-22, 33-34, 52, 53, 59, 61-66, 71, 76, 78-82, 104, 109-110, 142-146, 151, 153, 155, 163, 168, 169
Lee, Robert, 168
Lee, Shannon, 2, 4, 64, 78, 110, 111, 154-156, 168-172, 174
Lewis, Joe, 24-25, 30-31, 51
Little, John, 2-4, 9, 26, 30, 31, 38, 54, 141-164, 174, 177, 181, 183, 186, 188
Locke, Gary, 181
Logan, Bey, 147
Long Beach International Karate Championships, 20, 43, 130
Longstreet, 39, 47-48, 92, 115
Lo Wei, 50-51, 77

Madigan, Sean, 178
Marijuana, *see Cannabis*
Marlowe, 46, 59
Marshall, Adrian, 3, 80
Martial Arts Net Surfers, 171-172
Miao, Nora, 180
McQueen, Steve, 26, 73, 76, 175
Michael Collins, 137
Muscle and Fitness Magazine, 142

Norris, Chuck, 25, 30-31, 51, 179, 180
Nunchakus, 52, 53, 124

Oakland, 19, 21, 36, 62, 64, 101, 104
O'Neill, Martin, 100, 152-153, 157, 160, 164, 184-185

Parker, Ed, 20, 28, 43, 50, 85, 99, 127-129, 132
Plato, 152, 183
Polanski, Roman, 26
Poteet, Jerry, 25, 69, 82, 25, 69, 82
Presley, Elvis, 50, 80

Rapid Fire, 165
Rhee, Jhoon, 28, 32, 73, 181

Richardson, Burton, 10, 89-92, 96-98
Rome, 51, 99

St. Francis Xavier High School, 13
San Francisco, California, 11-12, 15, 105, 108, 111, 123, 157
Sato, Fred, 64, 72-73
Seattle, Washington, 2, 15-21, 34, 61-64, 67, 70, 71, 87, 88, 89, 101-102, 104, 169, 176, 181, 185
Sebring, Jay, 43
Shaw Brothers, 47, 49
Shaw, Run Run, 47, 49, 50, 80
Shunnarah, Alex, 186
Silliphant, Stirling, 26, 47
Star Wars, 175
Stone, Mike, 30
Strong, Patrick, 2, 18, 23, 30, 70, 87-89, 100, 176-177

Taekwondo, 7, 28, 73, 101, 112, 122, 171, 181
Tai Chi (martial art), 33, 120
Taoism, 8, 33-36
Tao of Jeet Kune Do, The, 81, 128, 140
Theosophical Society, 37
Thomas, Boyd, 8, 112-114
Thomas, Ted, 75, 180
Ting Pei, Betty, 59, 78-80
Torres, Richard, 94-95, 117
Triads, 53, 59

Ultimate Fighting Championship, 86
Universal Pictures, 82
University of Washington, 19
Uyehara, Mito, 177

Variety, 171

Walk in the Spring Rain, A, 46
Wall, Bob, 26, 51, 55-57, 88, 153
Ward, Burt, 45-46,
Warner Brothers, 146-147, 151, 153, 155, 157-158, 163, 171-172
Warrior, The, 9, 46, 52, 140, 172
Warrior Within, The, 9, 149, 184
Waugh, Darrin, 121-122
Way of the Dragon, The, 25, 31, 50-51, 55, 123, 127, 157, 179

Weintraub, Fred, 52, 168
West, Adam, 45
Williams, Van, 27, 44, 45, 79
Wing Chun, 13-14, 18, 19, 21-23, 25, 28, 33, 36, 87, 95, 101, 158-160, 177
Wilson, Andy, 174, 178
Wong, Ted, 71, 72, 109, 145, 157, 163, 171,
Wong, T. Y., 21
Wong Jack Man, 21-23, 36
Wong Shun Leung, 158-160

Woods, Dwight, 95-96
World War II, 67
Wrath of the Dragon: The Real Fights of Bruce Lee, 162
Wrecking Crew, The, 46

Yeung, Bolo, 174
Yip Man, 13, 15, 33, 75, 77, 158-160, 176, 177

Zen, 39-40

www.ingramcontent.com/pod-product-compliance
Lightning Source LLC
Chambersburg PA
CBHW070612170426
43200CB00012B/2663